Anonymous

Saint Mary's Chant-Book

A Collection of Anglican Chants by Ancient and Modern Composers

Anonymous

Saint Mary's Chant-Book
A Collection of Anglican Chants by Ancient and Modern Composers

ISBN/EAN: 9783337341039

Printed in Europe, USA, Canada, Australia, Japan

Cover: Foto ©Lupo / pixelio.de

More available books at **www.hansebooks.com**

PUBLISHED UNDER THE SANCTION OF
THE REVEREND THOMAS JACKSON, M.A.,
PREBENDARY OF ST. PAUL'S, AND RECTOR,
AND BY HIM AUTHORISED FOR USE IN THE PARISH CHURCH, STOKE NEWINGTON.

THE

SAINT MARY'S
CHANT·BOOK

A Collection of Anglican Chants

BY ANCIENT AND MODERN COMPOSERS

COMPILED, ARRANGED, AND EDITED FOR

The Choir of St. Mary's, Stoke Newington.

LONDON: NOVELLO, EWER & CO.,
1, BERNERS STREET (W.), AND 80 & 81, QUEEN STREET (E.C.)

IF distinguished services in a noble cause have any claim on public gratitude, I know not to whom I could more fitly inscribe this volume than to one by whose rare devotion the Choral Service at St. Mary's has attained its present high standard of usefulness and efficiency.

But it is in grateful remembrance of some of the happiest years of my life, as first Director of the Choir, that I dedicate this book to

MR. JAMES MATTHEWS,

CHOIRMASTER AND DIRECTOR OF THE CHOIR AT THE CHURCH OF ST. MARY.
STOKE NEWINGTON

NOTICE.

A LARGE number of the Chants in this Collection are Copyright, and cannot be reproduced without the permission of their Proprietors.

CONTENTS.

		PAGE
Preface...		vi
Index of Chants and Notices of Composers		ix
Chants for the Daily Psalms		2
,,	Proper Psalms	62
,,	Harvest Festival	74
,,	New Year's Eve	75
,,	Solemnization of Matrimony	76
,,	Burial of the Dead	77
,,	Benedictus	78
,,	Jubilate	79
,,	Magnificat	81
,.	Cantate Domino	84
	Nunc dimittis	86
,,	Quicunque vult	89

PREFACE.

The Book of Chants to the Daily Psalms, as sung at St. Mary's, has, with very few alterations, been regularly used since the year 1868.

Since that book was compiled, marvellous changes have taken place in the public taste in connection with Church Music, and, as a natural consequence, the Anglican Chant has been multiplied in such richness and variety that, at the request of the Choirmaster, the Editor has felt justified in supplementing his earlier efforts by a selection from the many beautiful compositions which have been placed at his disposal.

The Editor desires it may be understood that he lays no claim to the practised skill of a professional musician in the compilation and arrangement of this unpretending volume. Such a work would not have been commenced by him, and assuredly could never have been completed, without the generous assistance of the eminent musicians whose sterling compositions enrich its pages.

Amongst those who have given permission to use their respective copyrights, and for those written expressly for this work, his grateful thanks are especially due

To Dr. Stainer, M.A., for several beautiful Chants, and for his warm interest in the Editor's work.
To Sir George J. Elvey, Mus. Doc., for several original Chants.
To Mrs. Elvey, for three beautiful Chants by her late husband, Dr. Stephen Elvey.
To the late Sir John Goss, for several Chants, as well as for his courtesy to the Editor on repeated occasions.
To Professor G. A. Macfarren, Mus. Doc., for his sterling compositions.
To Dr. E. G. Monk and Professor the Rev. Sir F. A. Gore Ouseley, Bart., Mus. Doc., for their kind permission to make selections from their published works.
To the late Mr. Henry Smart, for Chants composed by him.
To Messrs. Novello, Ewer and Co., for their special permission to use several Chants of which they possess the copyright.

PREFACE. vii

To Mr. E. J. Hopkins, for Chants Nos. 119, 184.
To Dr. J. L. Hopkins, for No. 159.
To Mr. B. St. J. B. Joule, for Nos. 155, 175.
To Mr. James Turle, for the large collection of Chants which bear his name.
To Mr. Joseph Barnby, for Nos. 21, 131.
To Dr. J. F. Bridge, for No. 296.
To Messrs. Metzler, for Chants by the late Dr. Rimbault.
To Mr. Fountain Meen, for No. 283.
To the Rev. J. Troutbeck, M.A., for No. 26.
To the late Dr. S. S. Wesley, for No. 77.
To Dr. P. Armes, for Nos. 102, 336.
To Professor W. H. Monk, for No. 4.
To Dr. Garrett, for No. 78.
To Mr. John Foster, for Nos. 25, 61.
To Professor Sir H. S. Oakeley, for Nos. 113, 151.
To the Rev. F. A. J. Hervey, for No. 207.
To Messrs. R. Mills and Sons, for Chants by the late Dr. Crotch.
To Messrs. J. Masters and Co., for two Chants by the late W. Dyce.
To Mrs. Havergal, for Chants by her late husband, the Rev. W. H. Havergal.
To his friend, Arthur Henry Brown, his special gratitude is due for the large number of beautiful Chants, including the setting to the Quicunque vult, kindly composed by him expressly for this Collection.

And lastly, the Editor desires to acknowledge the personal courtesy of the Organist of St. Mary's, Mr. Henry T. Pringuer, as well as Mr. James Matthews, and Mr. Charles T. Johnson, of the Choir; the former for his careful revision of the proof-sheets for the press, besides much valuable assistance, and the latter for their important contributions no less than for their unwearied efforts to make his book the most perfect of its kind in existence. The Church that possesses the services of such men may well be envied, for they are rare.

The Editor has devoted earnest and especial care in the selection of those compositions which appeared devotional in expression, rich in vocal arrangement, and strictly ecclesiastical in character. As before, so now, the Collection consists of about an equal proportion of Single and Double Chants, and among them will be found a large number which are either original or now for the first time printed. The Venite has a change of Chant for every day in the month, and is set respectively in a key to insure easy transition to the Psalm which it precedes; whilst the Chants to the other Canticles have been considerably augmented. Very few Double Chants are adapted (the Editor regrets there should be any) to Psalms with an uneven number of verses. While unable to approve the indiscriminate use of Double Chants in the way so generally adopted, they are retained in one or two instances in deference to associations which he was unable to disregard.

Less than twenty years ago the introduction of the Choral Service was regarded with disfavour by the great mass of the people, and it was everywhere encountered by popular prejudice, yet the elevated tone of public worship has triumphantly attested its success in imparting beauty and devotion where everything was meanness and neglect. And if at the Parish Church the foresight and sagacity of the Rector were somewhat in advance of his time, the public mind has long since re-echoed the gratitude of an intelligent congregation for the Services which resound within its walls.

STOKE NEWINGTON,
 Advent, a.d. 1880.

INDEX OF CHANTS

AND

NOTICES OF COMPOSERS.

* *The same Chant in different keys.*

NAME OF COMPOSER.	SINGLE.	DOUBLE.
ALCOCK, JOHN, Mus. Doc., Oxon., Organist of Lichfield Cathedral. Born, 1715; died, 1806.	A♭, 300	
ALDRICH, Rev. HENRY, D.D., Dean of Christ Church Cathedral, Oxford. Born, 1647; died, 1710.	*A, 118 *A♭, 251 F, 339	
ALLEN, W., London	B♭, 37	
ARMES, PHILIP, Mus. Doc., Oxon., Organist of Durham Cathedral.	A♭, 102 E, 336	
ATTWOOD, THOMAS. Born, 1767. Organist of St. Paul's Cathedral, 1795. Pupil of Mozart. Succeeded Dr. Dupuis as Composer to the Chapel Royal. Mendelssohn was the guest of Attwood at Norwood during his visit to England in 1832. Died, 1838, and was buried under the organ at St. Paul's Cathedral.		E, 48
AYLWARD, THEODORE, Mus. Doc., Organist of Windsor. Died, 1801.	D, 32, 98, 278	
BARNBY, JOSEPH, Precentor of Eton College	E, 131, 191, 277, 281 F, 21, 110	
BARROW, ISAAC, Gentleman of the Chapel Royal. Died, 1789.	*E, 43 *E♭, 221	
BARRY, C. A., Sydenham	F, 299	
BATES, GEORGE, Organist of Ripon Cathedral	...	G, 319
BATTISHILL, JONATHAN, Organist of Christ Church, Newgate Street, London. Born, 1738; died, 1801.	A, 200 D, 74, 135 G, 313	A m, 24, 116, 229
BAYLEY	...	E♭, 101, 127, 243
BEETHOVEN, L. V. Born, 1772; died, 1827	...	C m, 2 9, 232
BLOW, JOHN, Mus. Doc., Organist of Westminster Abbey, 1669, and Master of Henry Purcell, in whose favour he resigned in 1680. Born, 1648; died, 1708.	E, 45, 237 E m, 44, 80, 236, 280	
BOYCE, WILLIAM, Mus. Doc., Organist of the Chapel Royal. Born, 1710; died, 1779.		F, 297
BRIDGE, J. F., Mus. Doc., Oxon., Organist of Westminster Abbey.		A, 296

NAME OF COMPOSER.	SINGLE.	DOUBLE.
BROWN, ARTHUR HENRY, Organist of Brentwood, Essex	*A, 16, 240, 276 *B♭, 163 *A, 172 *A♭, 253 A, 204 A, 342 *A, 214 *G, 242 G, 311 A, 244 D, 70 E, 337 E♭, 142 E♭, 304 F, 331	
BYRDE, WILLIAM, Organist of Lincoln Cathedral, afterwards Gentleman of the Chapel Royal. Pupil of Tallis. Born, 1538; died, 1623.	G, 7, 76	
CAMIDGE, JOHN, Mus. Doc., Organist of York Minster. Died, 1859.	A, 89, 192 A♭, 270	
CAMIDGE, MATTHEW, Organist of York Minster. Born, 1764; died, 1844.		*E, 171 *E♭, 181 E m, 84, 187
CHARD, WILLIAM, Mus. Doc., Organist of Winchester Cathedral. Born, 1765; died, 1849.		A, 287
CHARLESWORTH, J., Hereford	F, 305	
COOKE, ROBERT, Organist of Westminster Abbey. Died, 1814.		G, 288 G, 289
COOPER, GEORGE. Born, 1820. Pupil of Attwood, for whom, when only 11 years of age, in Mendelssohn's presence, he took the Service at St. Paul's at one of the Festivals of the Sons of the Clergy. Assistant Organist of St. Paul's at Attwood's death. In 1843 he succeeded his father at St. Sepulchre's, and was Organist of the Chapel Royal. Died, 1876.		G, 90, 121
COOPER, J. T., Organist of Christ Church, Newgate Street. Died, 1878.	A m, 17, 146	
CORFE, JOSEPH, Organist of Salisbury Cathedral. Born, 1740; died, 1820.	G, 307	
CORFE, A. T., son of the preceding, and Organist of Salisbury Cathedral. Born, 1773.	F, 335	
CROFT, WILLIAM, Mus. Doc., Oxon. Pupil of Dr. Blow. Organist of Westminster Abbey. Born, 1677; died, 1727.	B m, 69, 136	

NAME OF COMPOSER.	SINGLE.	DOUBLE.
CROTCH, WILLIAM, Mus. Doc., Oxon. Born, 1775. Professor of Music at Oxford University, and Principal of the Royal Academy of Music, London. Died, 1847.	A, 18, 189 A m, 190, 206, 275 A♭, 100 B, 86 *D, 72. 211. 259 *E♭, 40 G, 52, 226 G, 340	G, 290 G, 317
DEARLE, EDWARD, Mus. Doc., Organist at Newark		G, 293
DUPUIS, THOMAS SAUNDERS, Mus. Doc. Succeeded Dr. Boyce as Organist and Composer to the Chapel Royal. Born, 1773; died, 1796.	G, 314	D♭, 94 E, 87
DYCE, WILLIAM, London, R.A. Editor of "Gregorian and other Chants."	E♭, 125, 194, 223 F, 36, 166	
ELVEY, Sir GEORGE J., Mus. Doc., Oxon. Born, 1816. Succeeded Skeats as Organist of St. George's Chapel, Windsor, 1835.	B♭, 111 C, 115, 257 C, 153, 261 D, 315	G, 201 A, 35, 248, 258
ELVEY, STEPHEN, Mus. Doc. Brother of the preceding. Born, 1805. Organist of New College, Oxford. Died, 1860.	A, 329 B♭, 63	E, 134, 205 F, 23
FARRANT, RICHARD. Born, 1530. Gentleman of the Chapel Royal during the reigns of Edward VI., Mary, and Elizabeth; Organist of St. George's Chapel, Windsor, 1564. Died, 1580.	F, 306	
FELTON, Rev. WILLIAM, Mus. Bac. Custos of the Vicars Choral of Hereford Cathedral. Died, 1769.	*E, 132 *E♭, 57, 106	
FIELDING, S.	A♭, 341	
FLINTOFT, Rev. L. Composer of the beautiful Chant founded upon a tune in "Playford's Psalter," 1671. Died, 1780.	...	G m, 53, 56, 241
FOSTER, JOHN. Gentleman of the Chapel Royal, and Vicar Choral of Westminster Abbey.	E, 61, 117	E, 25, 88
FUSSELL, PETER, Organist of Winchester Cathedral. Died, 1790.	G, 152, 216, 268	
GARRETT, GEORGE M., Mus. Doc., Organist of St. John's College, Cambridge.	*E, 193 *E♭, 78	
GAUNTLETT, HENRY JOHN, Mus. Doc. An eminent Organist and Composer, as well as an important contributor to the best musical literature of his time. Died, 1877.	...	G, 294

NAME OF COMPOSER.	SINGLE.	DOUBLE.
GIBBONS, Dr. C., Organist of the Chapel Royal and Westminster Abbey. Died, 1676.	G, 99, 235	
GOLDWIN, JOHN, Organist of St. George's Chapel, Windsor. Died, 1819.	G m, 39, 176	
GOODENOUGH, Rev. ROBERT PHILIP, M.A., Prebendary of York. Died, 1826.		A♮, 65, 222
GOODSON, RICHARD, Mus. Bac., Organist of Christ Church Cathedral, Oxford, and Professor of Music at the University, 1682. Died, 1717.	B, 130	
GOSS, Sir JOHN, Mus. Doc. Born at Fareham, 1800. Succeeded Attwood as Organist of St. Paul's Cathedral in 1838. Resigned in 1872. Appointed Composer to the Chapel Royal in 1856. Died, 1880.	*A, 133, 147 *A♮, 5 A, 158 *A, 62 *A♭, 107 D, 34 E, 85, 239	E, 149, 178 F, 167 G, 316
GREENE, MAURICE, Mus. Doc., Organist of St. Paul's Cathedral in succession to Dr. Croft. Born, 1696; died, 1755.	G, 55	
HANDEL, GEORGE FREDERIC. Born, 1685; died, 1759		G, 292
HARRIS, J. T., Organist of Manchester Cathedral. Born, 1799; died, 1869.		E, 46
HAVERGAL, Rev. W. H., M.A., Honorary Canon of Worcester Cathedral. Devoted an earnest and valuable life to the cause of Church music. Died, 1870.	B♭, 11 *E, 213 *E♮ 144	A, 282 E♭, 64, 105
HAYES, PHILIP, Mus. Doc., Oxon., Organist of Magdalen College, Oxford. Born, 1739; died, 1797.	F, 49	
HAYES, WILLIAM, Mus. Doc., Oxon., Organist of Christ Church Cathedral, Oxford. Born, 1707; died, 1777.	E, 327	F, 321
HEATHCOTE, Rev. G., Archdeacon of Winchester. Died, 1829.		B♮, 323
HENLEY, Rev. PHOCION, M.A. Died, 1778 ...	...	E, 291
HERVEY, Rev. F. A. J., Domestic Chaplain to the Prince of Wales, and Rector of Sandringham, Norfolk.	E, 207	
HINDLE, JOHN, Mus. Bac. Died, 1781 ...	A, 210	
HINE, WILLIAM. Died, 1739	G, 67	
HOPKINS, EDWARD J., Organist of the Temple Church, London.	E, 119	*D, 184 *D♮, 96
HOPKINS, J. L., Mus. Doc., Organist of Trinity College, Cambridge. Died, 1873.		D, 159, 215, 271
HUMPHREYS, PELHAM. Born, 1647. Succeeded Cooke as Master of the boys and Gentleman of the Chapel Royal, 1672. Died, 1674.	C, 8, 217, 273	

NAME OF COMPOSER.	SINGLE.	DOUBLE.
JACOBS, Rev. WILLIAM, M.A., Chaplain of New College, Oxford.		B♭, 169
JOULE, B. ST. J. B., Hon. Organist St. Peter's Church, Manchester.	E, 328 F, 333	G, 155 G, 175
KELWAY, T., Organist of St. Martin's-in-the-Fields, London. Died, 1750.	D, 29, 75 G, 308 G m, 6	
KEMPTON, T., London	B♭, 124	
KINKEE, F., London	B♭, 164	
LANGDON, RICHARD, Mus. Bac., Organist of Armagh Cathedral. Died, 1798.		F, 295
LAWES, H. Died, 1662		C, 168
LEE, WILLIAM	E, 27 G, 183	
LONGDON, T., London	C, 230	
MACFARREN, GEORGE ALEXANDER, Mus. Doc. Born, 1812. Principal of the Royal Academy of Music, London, Professor of Music at Cambridge University.	*A, 28 *A♭, 15 A, 42 A m, 19, 148 B♭, 20 B♭, 109	
MARTIN, R. A. Died, 1867		G, 224, 326
MATTHEWS, JAMES, Director of the Choir of St. Mary's, Stoke Newington, London.		G, 188, 250 A, 322 E, 285
MEDLEY, Right Rev. Dr.	A, 185	
MEEN, FOUNTAIN, Organist of St. Mary's, Stoke Newington, 1870 to 1879.		D, 283
MONK, EDWIN GEORGE, Mus. Doc., Organist of York Minster.	A, 47, 71, 238 A♭, 93 C, 255 E♭, 2, 161 G, 303 G, 310	
MONK, WILLIAM HENRY, Professor of Vocal Music at King's College, London.	E♭, 4, 66, 233	
MORLEY, WILLIAM, Gentleman of the Chapel Royal. Died, 1738.		D m, 31, 97
MORNINGTON, Earl of, an accomplished Musician and Composer of some beautiful Glees. Died, 1781.		*D, 114 *D♭, 265

NAME OF COMPOSER.	SINGLE.	DOUBLE.
NARES, JAMES, Mus. Doc. Born, 1715. Organist of York Minster. Succeeded Travers at the Chapel Royal, 1758. Died, 1783.	A, 30, 60	A m, 231
OAKELEY, Sir HERBERT STANLEY, M.A., Mus. Doc., Professor of Music at Edinburgh.	*D, 151 *E, 173	G, 113
OUSELEY, Rev. Sir F. A. GORE, Bart., Mus. Doc., Oxon., Professor of Music at Oxford University, and Precentor of Hereford Cathedral.	B♭, 54 D, 68 *D, 267 *E♭, 103 E♭, 120, 269 G, 79	
PATTEN, W.		E♭, 12
PRINGUER, HENRY T., Mus. Bac., Oxon., Organist of St. Mary's, Stoke Newington.	B♭, 343	D, 325
PURCELL, DANIEL, brother of Henry Purcell. Died, 1717	*A♭, 126 *G, 123, 260	
PURCELL, HENRY, born in London, 1658. Organist of Westminster Abbey, 1680, and of the Chapel Royal, 1682. Died, 1695, and was buried in Westminster Abbey. The name of Henry Purcell will ever be held in reverence by all sterling musicians.	A, 298	*F m, 129 *G m, 225
PURCELL, THOMAS, uncle of Henry Purcell, Gentleman of the Chapel Royal. Died, 1682.	G, 83, 195, 203 G m, 82, 196, 202	
RANDALL, JOHN, Mus. Doc., Professor of Music at Cambridge University. Died, 1755.		E♭, 58
RIMBAULT, E. F., LL.D. Born, 1816. A composer, an editor, and a musical critic of high attainments. Died, 1876.	F, 140, 254, 262 F, 334	
ROBINSON, JOHN, Organist of Westminster Abbey. Died, 1762.		E, 286 E♭, 318
ROGERS, Sir JOHN LEMAN, Bart., President of the Madrigal Society, and an accomplished musician. Born, 1775; died, 1847.	G, 33, 92, 272, 279	A♭, 3, 95, 154 E♭, 14, 156
RUSSELL, WILLIAM, Mus. Bac., Organist of the Foundling Hospital, London. Born, 1777; died, 1873.	F, 112, 256	G, 150
SAVAGE, WILLIAM, Gentleman of the Chapel Royal. Died, 1789.	C, 165	
SCOTCH CHANT...	G, 309	
SIXTH TONE	F, 332	
SMART, HENRY, Organist of St. Pancras Church, London. Born, 1812; died, 1879.	A, 212	*B, 179 *C, 22 E, 81

INDEX OF CHANTS AND NOTICES OF COMPOSERS.

NAME OF COMPOSER.	SINGLE.	DOUBLE.
SMITH, JOHN STAFFORD, Organist, Chapel Royal. Born, 1750; died, 1837.		A♭, 324
SPOHR, LUDWIG. Born, 1784; died, 1859	...	F, 284
STAINER, JOHN, M.A., Mus. Doc., Oxon., Organist of St. Paul's Cathedral, London.	*B m, 73 ♯ C m, 13, 59 D, 122, 199, 227	
STEPHENS, C. E., London ...	C, 228	
STEVENSON, R. H.	A, 160, 198	
STEWART, Sir R. P., Professor of Music, Trinity College, Dublin.	G, 301	
TALLIS, THOMAS. Born, 1520. Gentleman of the Chapel Royal in the reigns of Henry VIII., Edward VI., and Mary. Organist of the Chapel Royal in the reign of Elizabeth. Died, 1585.	C, 145, 220 F, 138 F, 344	
TROUTBECK, Rev. J., M.A., Priest in Ordinary to the Queen, and Canon of Westminster.		A, 26 A♭, 264
TUCKER, Rev. WILLIAM, Precentor of Westminster Abbey in the reign of Charles II. Died, 1678.	A♭, 1	
TURLE, JAMES, Organist of Westminster Abbey	F, 338 G, 302 G, 312	D, 51, 249 D m, 50 *D, 91 *D♭, 252 F, 128 F, 186 G, 141, 266
TURNER, WILLIAM, Mus. Doc., Gentleman of the Chapel Royal. Born, 1652; died, 1740.	B♭, 41	
TURTON, Right Rev. THOMAS, Bishop of Ely. Born, 1780; died, 1864.	A, 170	
WEBBE, SAMUEL, a celebrated writer of English Glees. Died, 1817.	A, 177 E, 197	
WELDON, JOHN, succeeded Dr. Blow as Organist to the Chapel Royal, 1708. Died, 1736.	G m, 162	
WESLEY, SAMUEL, the greatest Organ-player of his time. Celebrated for his wonderful powers as an extemporaneous performer. Born, 1766; died, 1815.	F, 330	G, 320
WESLEY, SAMUEL SEBASTIAN, Mus. Doc., Oxon., Son of Samuel Wesley. Successively Organist of the Cathedrals of Hereford, Exeter, Winchester, and Gloucester. Born, 1810; died, 1876.	G m, 77, 208, 234	
WHITTINGTON, C. J., Manchester	...	G, 38, 180
WOODWARD, G., London	B♭, 139	
WOODWARD, RICHARD, Mus. Doc., Organist of Christ Church Cathedral, Dublin. Died, 1778.	...	D♭, 263

FIRST DAY.

MORNING PRAYER.

1.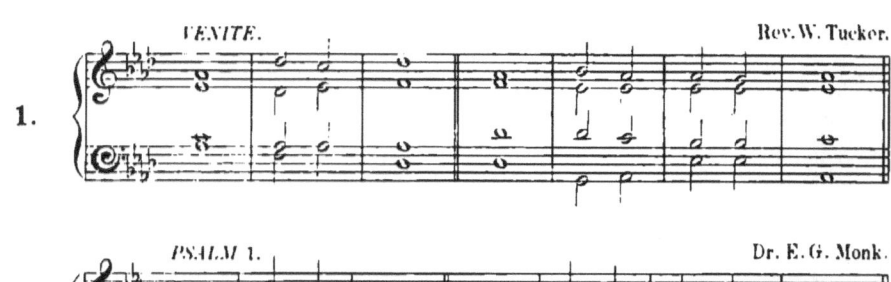

2.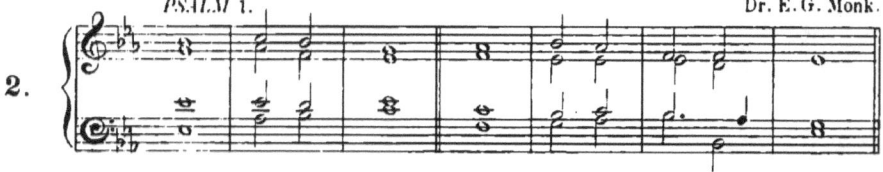

3.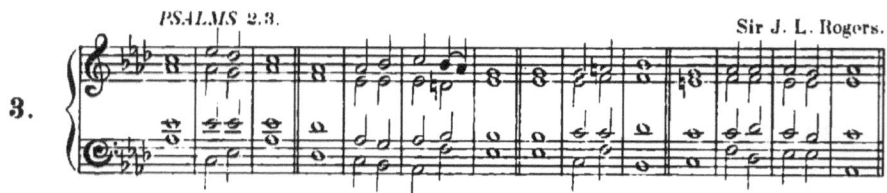

4.

5.

FIRST DAY.

EVENING PRAYER.

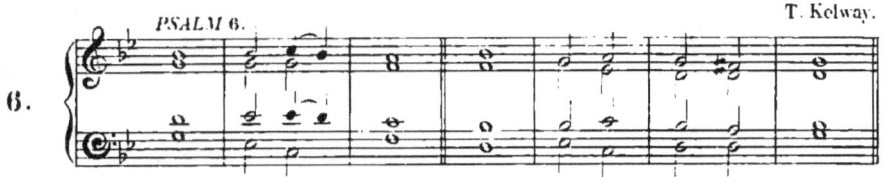

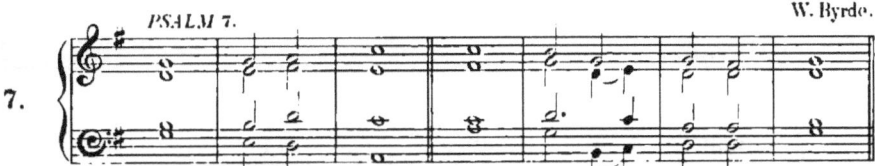

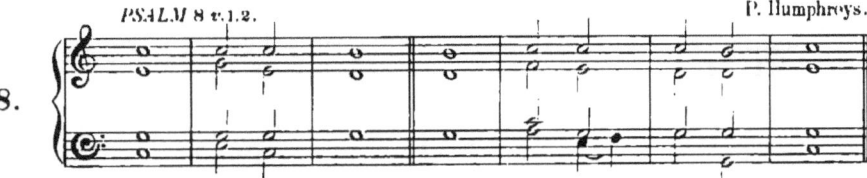

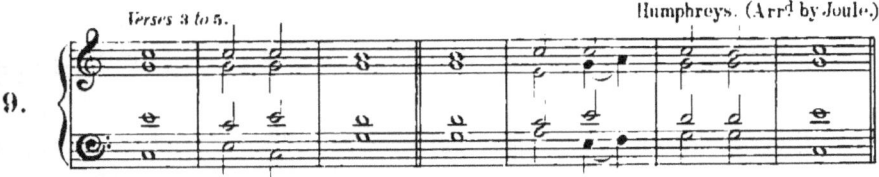

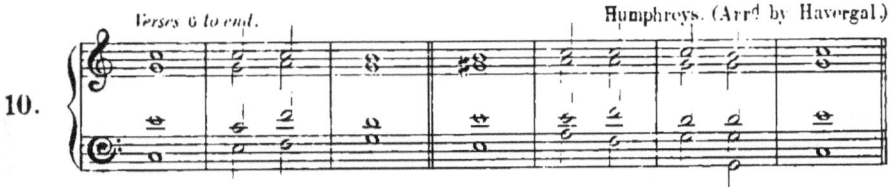

SECOND DAY.

MORNING PRAYER.

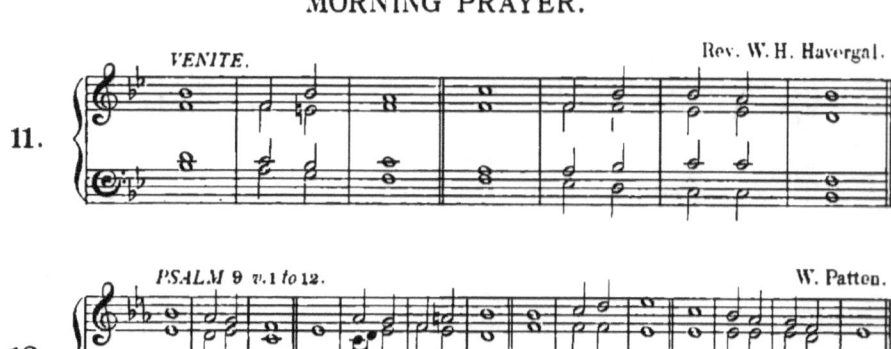

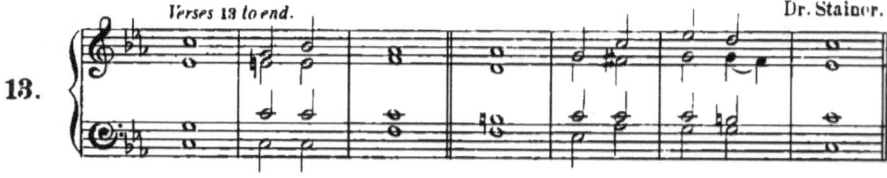

SECOND DAY.

EVENING PRAYER.

16. PSALM 12.   A. H. Brown.

17. PSALM 13 v. 1 to 4.   J. T. Cooper.

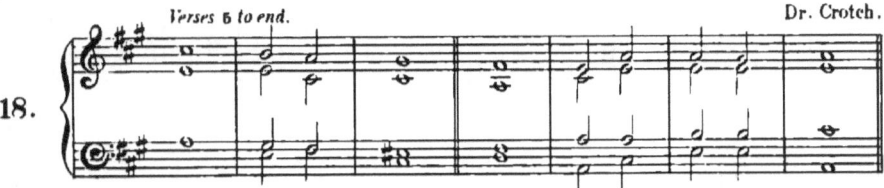

18. Verses 5 to end.   Dr. Crotch.

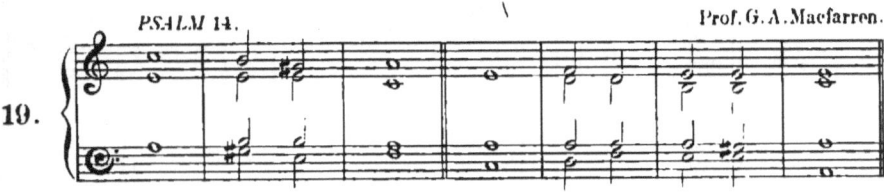

19. PSALM 14.   Prof. G. A. Macfarren.

THIRD DAY.

MORNING PRAYER.

20.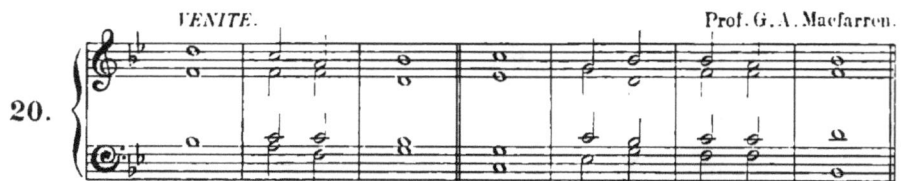
VENITE. — Prof. G. A. Macfarren.

21.
PSALM 15. — J. Barnby.

22.
PSALM 16. — Henry Smart.

23.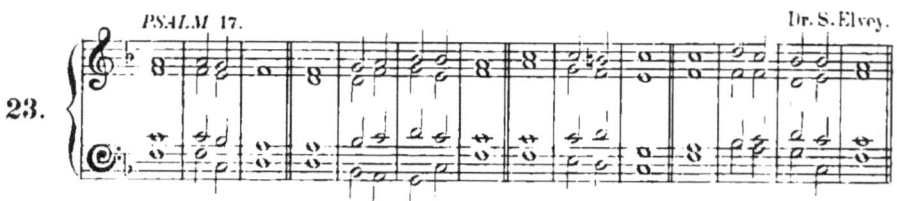
PSALM 17. — Dr. S. Elvey.

THIRD DAY.

EVENING PRAYER.

24.
J. Battishill.
PSALM 18 v. 1 to 16.

25.
John Foster.
Verses 17 to 30.

26.
Rev. J. Troutbeck.
Verses 31 to end.

FOURTH DAY.

MORNING PRAYER.

27. VENITE. W. Lee.
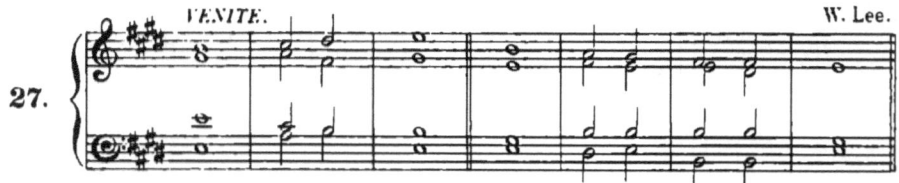

28. PSALM 19. Prof. G. A. Macfarren.

29. PSALM 20. T. Kelway.
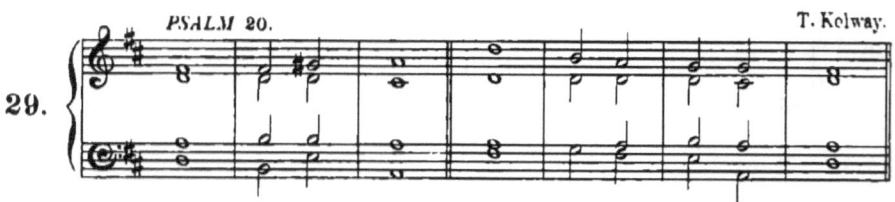

30. PSALM 21. Dr. J. Nares.
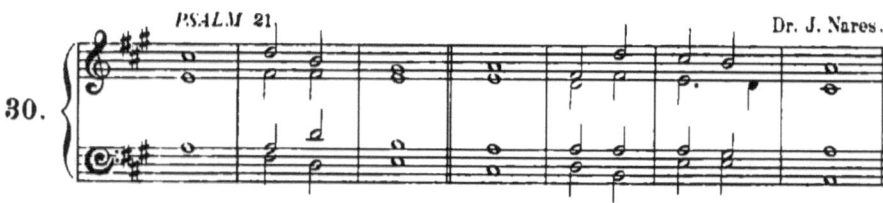

FOURTH DAY.

EVENING PRAYER.

31. PSALM 22. v. 1 to 22.   W. Morley B.Mus.

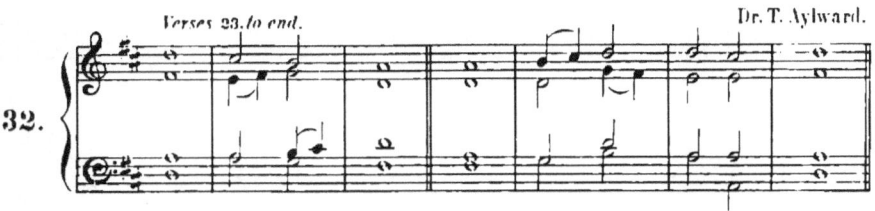

32. Verses 23. to end.   Dr. T. Aylward.

33. PSALM 23.   Sir J.L. Rogers.

FIFTH DAY.

MORNING PRAYER.

34. VENITE. — Sir John Goss.

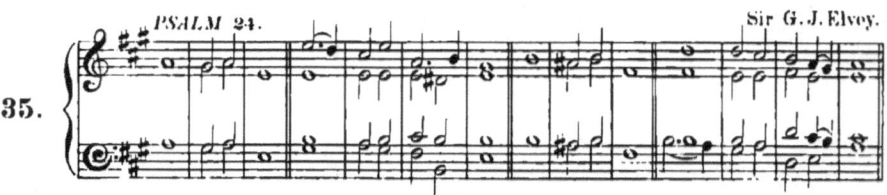

35. PSALM 24. — Sir G. J. Elvey.

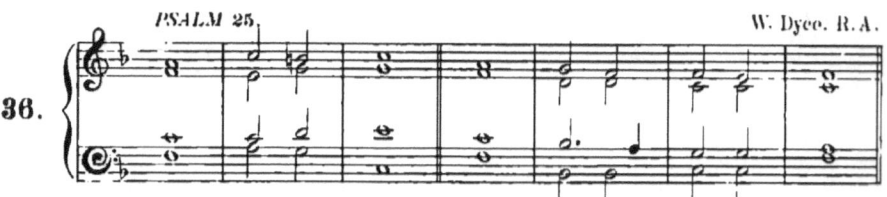

36. PSALM 25. — W. Dyce, R.A.

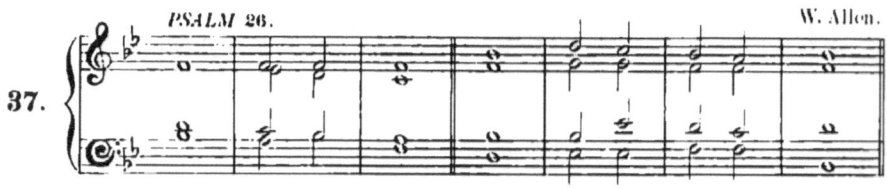

37. PSALM 26. — W. Allen.

FIFTH DAY.

EVENING PRAYER.

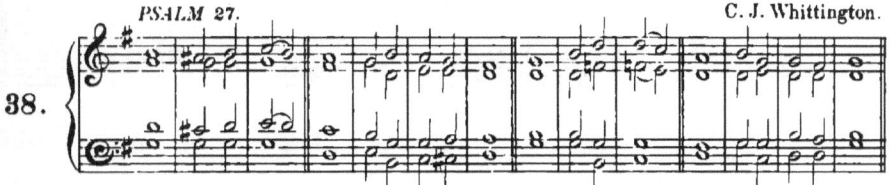

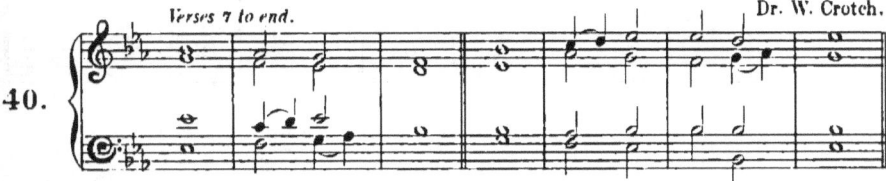

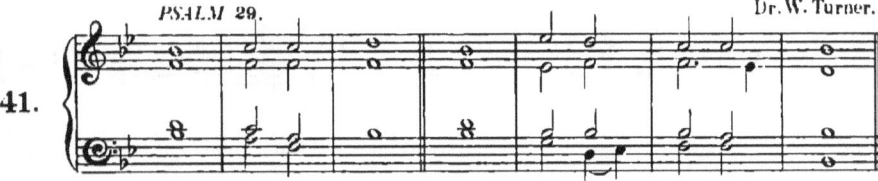

SIXTH DAY.

MORNING PRAYER.

42.
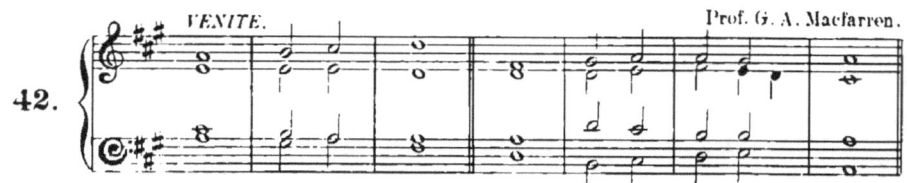
VENITE.   Prof. G. A. Macfarren.

43.
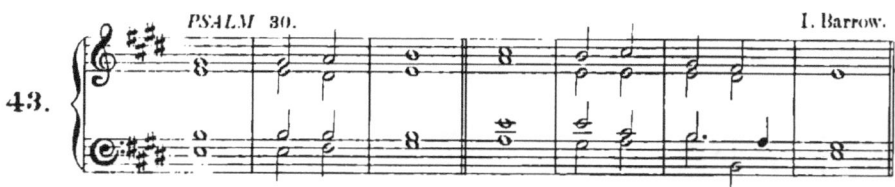
PSALM 30.   I. Barrow.

44.

PSALM 31 v.1 to 22.   Dr. J. Blow.

45.

Verses 23 to end.   Dr. J. Blow.

SIXTH DAY.

EVENING PRAYER.

46. PSALM 32. J. T. Harris.

47. PSALM 33. Dr. E. G. Monk.

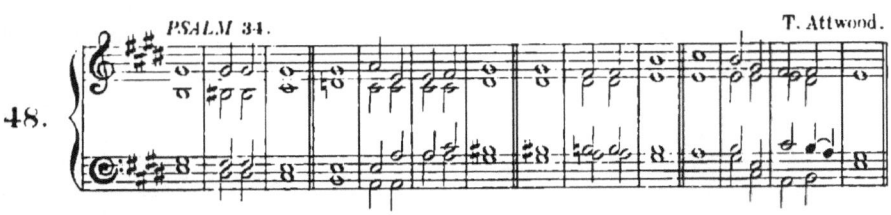

48. PSALM 34. T. Attwood.

SEVENTH DAY.

MORNING PRAYER.

49.

50.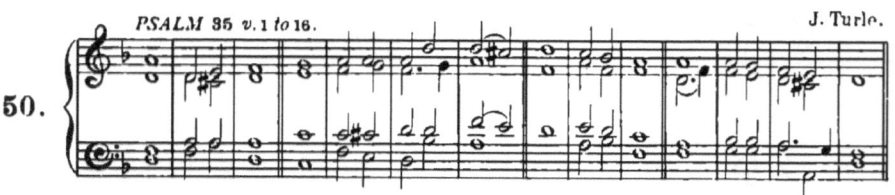

51.

52.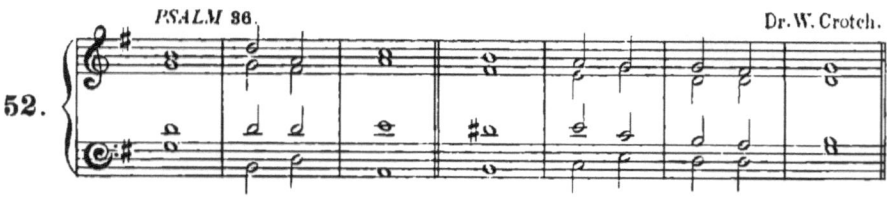

SEVENTH DAY.

EVENING PRAYER.

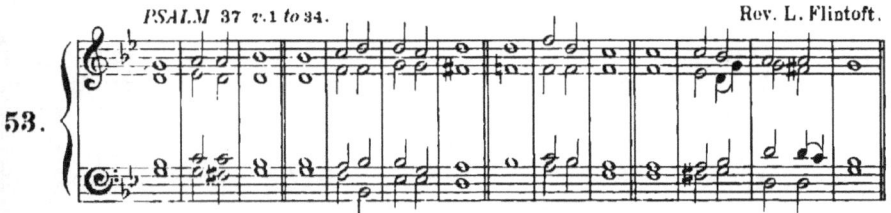

53. PSALM 37 v.1 to 34.   Rev. L. Flintoft.

54. Verses 35 to end.   Rev. Sir F. A. Gore Ouseley.

EIGHTH DAY.

MORNING PRAYER.

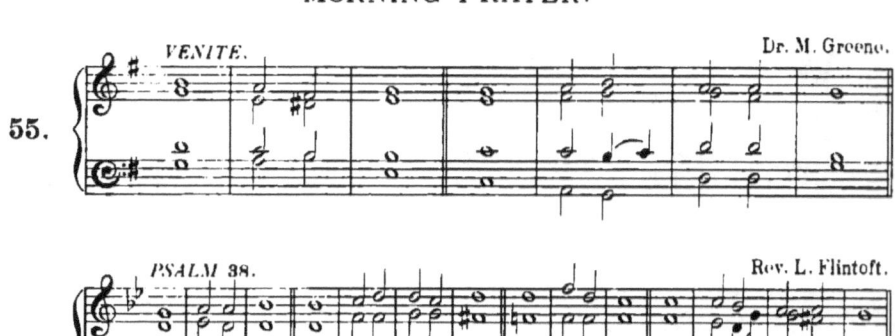

55. VENITE. — Dr. M. Greene.

56. PSALM 38. — Rev. L. Flintoft.

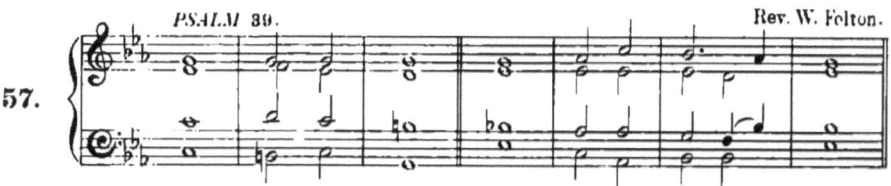

57. PSALM 39. — Rev. W. Felton.

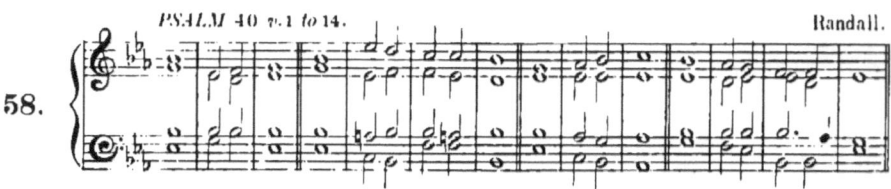

58. PSALM 40 v. 1 to 14. — Randall.

59. Verses 15 to 21. — Dr. Stainer.

Gloria to Nº 58.

EIGHTH DAY.

EVENING PRAYER.

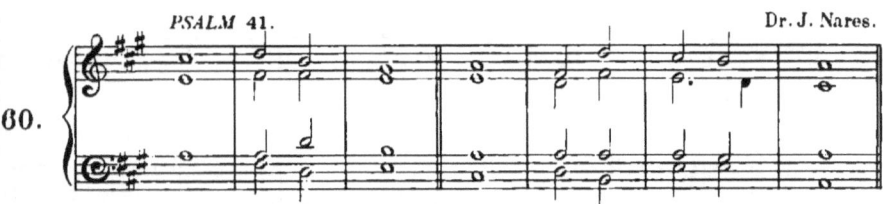

60. PSALM 41. — Dr. J. Nares.

61. PSALM 42. — John Foster.

62. PSALM 43. — Sir John Goss.

NINTH DAY.

MORNING PRAYER.

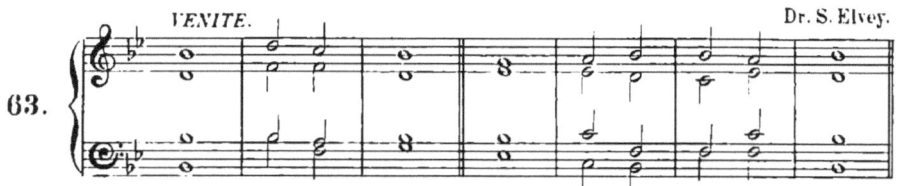

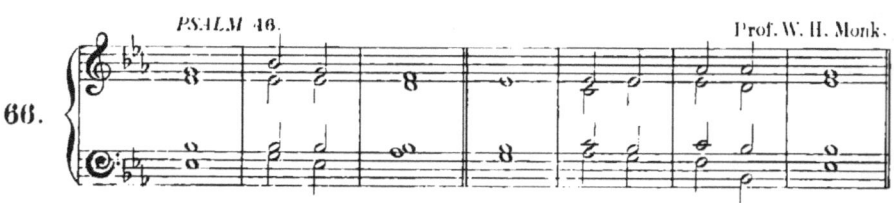

NINTH DAY.

EVENING PRAYER.

67. PSALM 47. W. Hine.

68. PSALM 48. Rev. Sir F. A. Gore Ouseley.

69. PSALM 49. Dr. W. Croft.

TENTH DAY.

MORNING PRAYER.

TENTH DAY.

EVENING PRAYER.

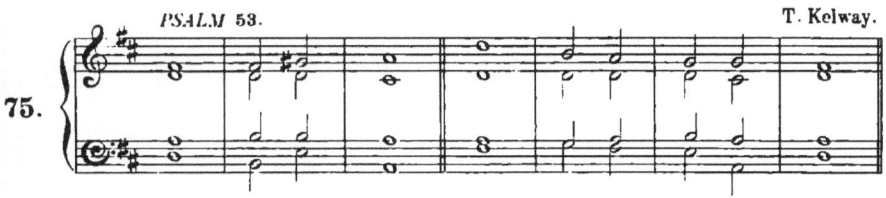

75. PSALM 53. — T. Kelway.

76. PSALM 54. — W. Byrde.

77. PSALM 55 v. 1 to 16. — Dr. S. S. Wesley.

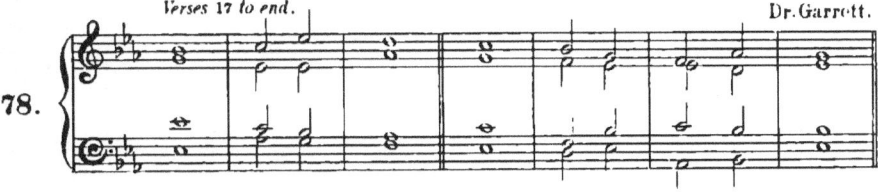

78. Verses 17 to end. — Dr. Garrett.

ELEVENTH DAY.

MORNING PRAYER.

79.
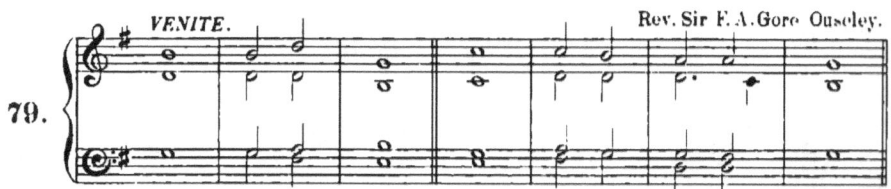
VENITE. — Rev. Sir F. A. Gore Ouseley.

80.
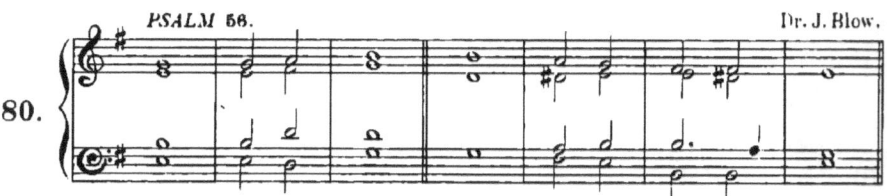
PSALM 56. — Dr. J. Blow.

81.
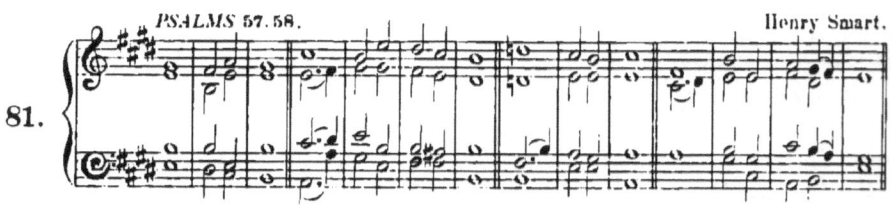
PSALMS 57. 58. — Henry Smart.

ELEVENTH DAY.

EVENING PRAYER.

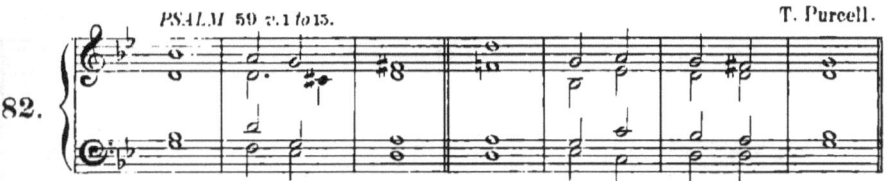

82. PSALM 59 v.1 to 15. T. Purcell.

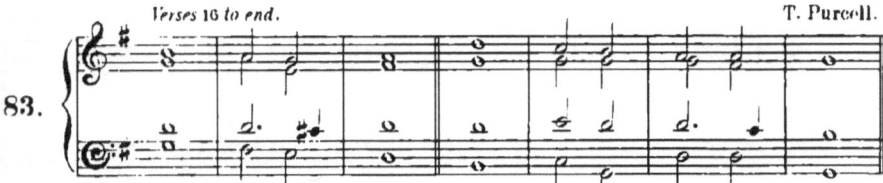

83. Verses 16 to end. T. Purcell.

84. PSALM 60. M. Camidge.

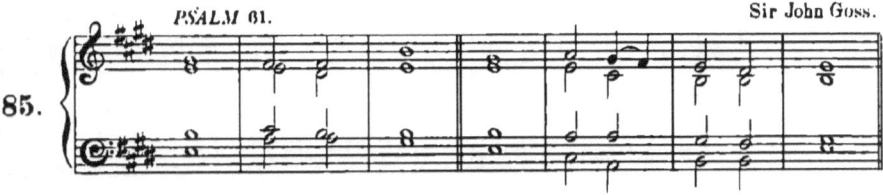

85. PSALM 61. Sir John Goss.

TWELFTH DAY.

MORNING PRAYER.

86.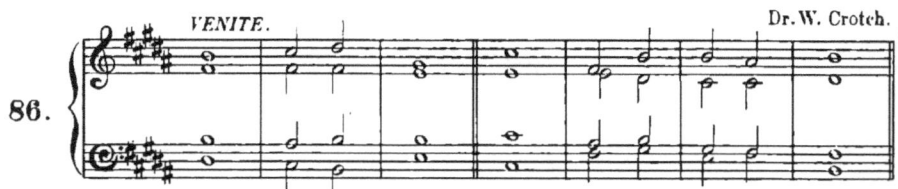
VENITE. — Dr. W. Crotch.

87.
PSALM 62. — Dr. T. S. Dupuis.

88.
PSALM 63. — John Foster.

89.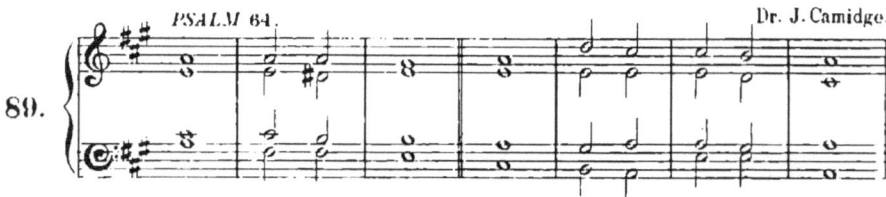
PSALM 64. — Dr. J. Camidge.

TWELFTH DAY.

EVENING PRAYER.

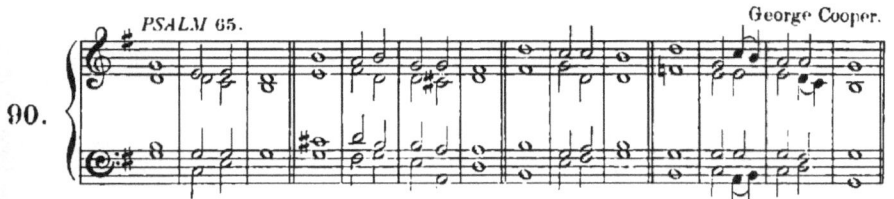

90. PSALM 65. George Cooper.

91. PSALM 66. J. Turle.

92. PSALM 67. Sir J. L. Rogers.

THIRTEENTH DAY.

MORNING PRAYER.

93.

VENITE. — Dr. E. G. Monk.

94.
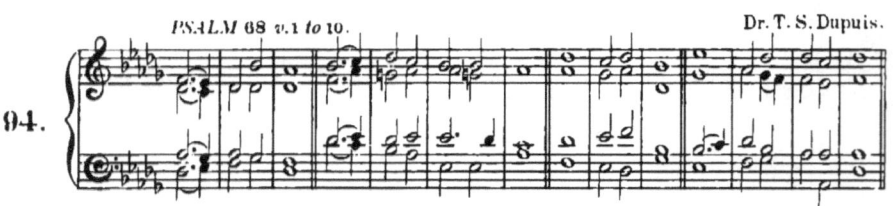
PSALM 68 v. 1 to 10. — Dr. T. S. Dupuis.

95.

Verses 11 to 20. — Sir J. L. Rogers.

96.

Verses 21 to end. — E. J. Hopkins.

THIRTEENTH DAY.

EVENING PRAYER.

97. PSALM 69 v. 1 to 30.   W. Morley. B. Mus.

98. Verses 31 to end.   Dr. T. Aylward.

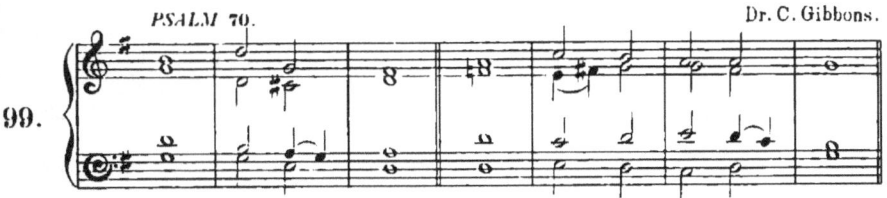

99. PSALM 70.   Dr. C. Gibbons.

FOURTEENTH DAY.

MORNING PRAYER.

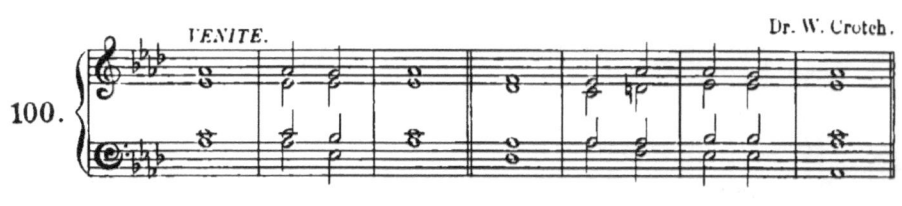

100. *VENITE.* — Dr. W. Crotch.

101. PSALM 71. — Bayley.

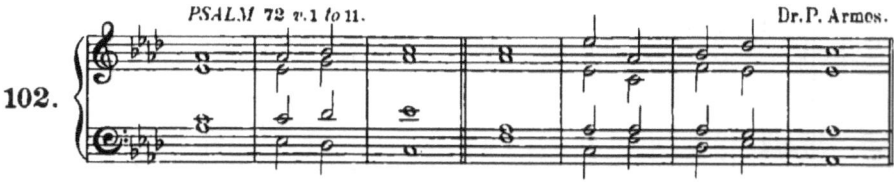

102. PSALM 72 v. 1 to 11. — Dr. P. Armes.

103. Verses 12 to 16. — Rev. Sir F. A. Gore Ouseley.

104. Verses 17 to end. — Dr. P. Armes.

FOURTEENTH DAY.

EVENING PRAYER.

105. PSALM 73. — Rev. W. H. Havergal.

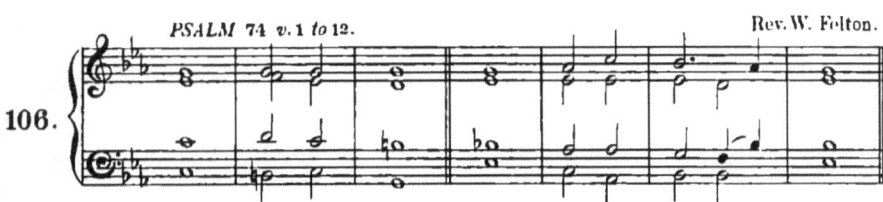

106. PSALM 74 v. 1 to 12. — Rev. W. Felton.

107. Verses 13 to 18. — Sir John Goss.

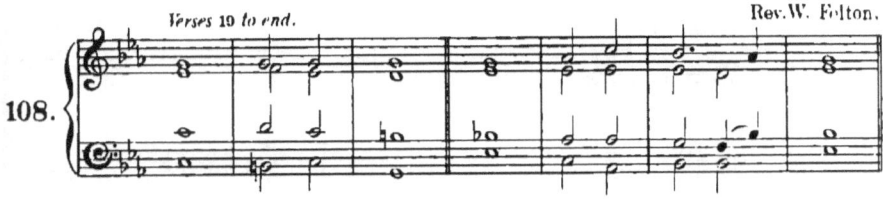

108. Verses 19 to end. — Rev. W. Felton.

FIFTEENTH DAY.

MORNING PRAYER.

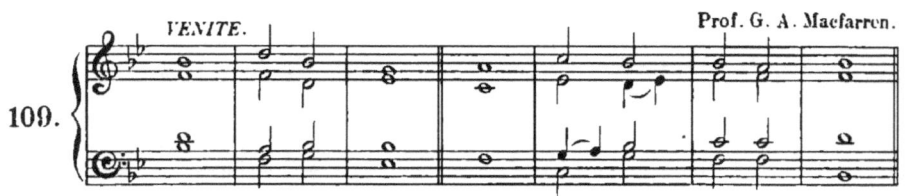

109. VENITE. Prof. G. A. Macfarren.

110. PSALM 75. J. Barnby.

111. PSALM 76. Sir G. Elvey.

112. PSALM 77. W. Russell.

FIFTEENTH DAY.

EVENING PRAYER.
Quadruple Chant.

113. PSALM 78 v. 1 to 32 and 53 to end. — Sir H. S. Oakeley.
+) Verse 73 commences here.

114. Verses 33 to 52. — Earl of Mornington.
Return to Oakeley at v. 53.

SIXTEENTH DAY.

MORNING PRAYER.

VENITE. Sir G. Elvey.

115.

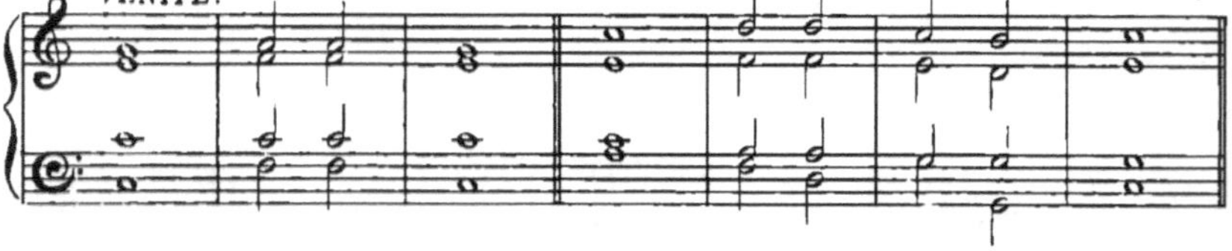

PSALM 79. J. Battishill.

116.

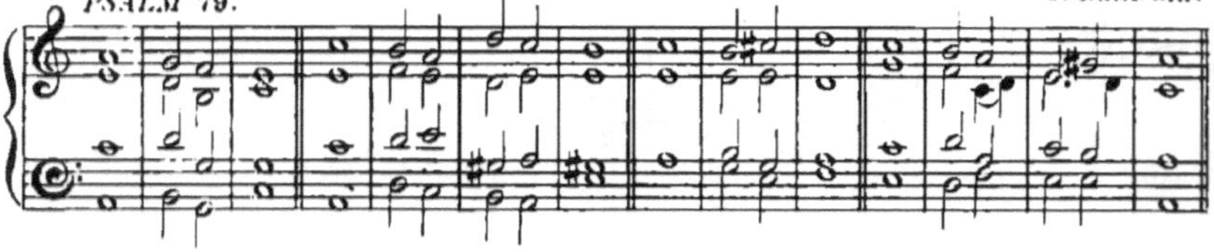

PSALM 80. John Foster.

117.

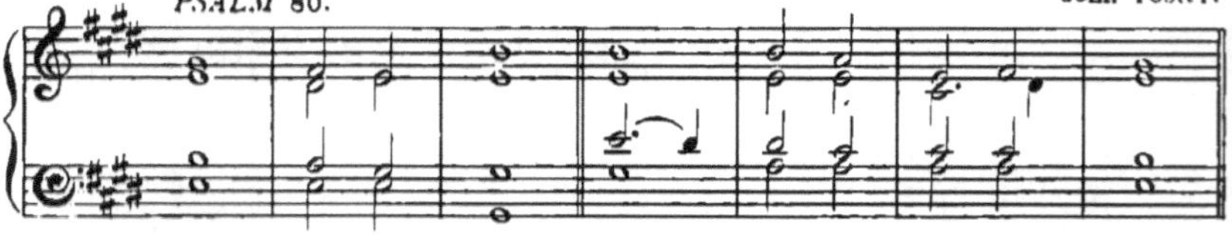

PSALM 81 *v.* 1 *to* 11. Dr. H. Aldrich.

118.

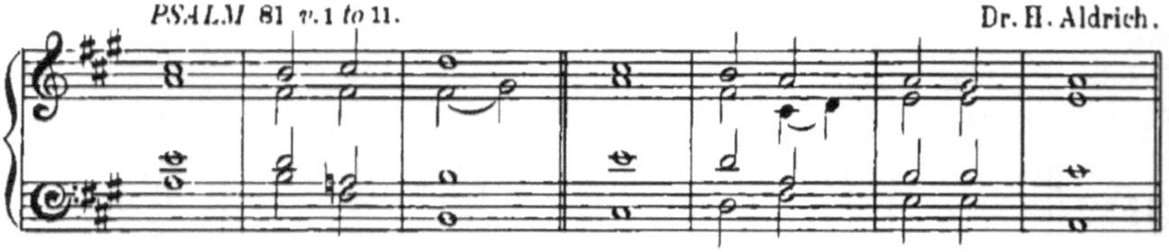

Verses 12 *to end.* F. J. Hopkins.

119.

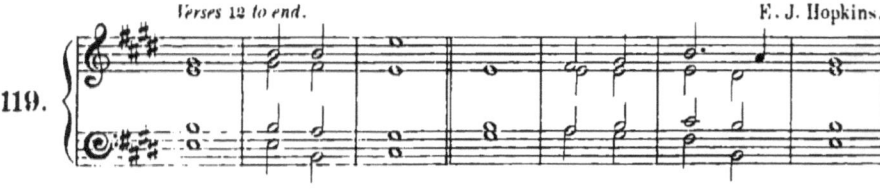

SIXTEENTH DAY.

EVENING PRAYER.

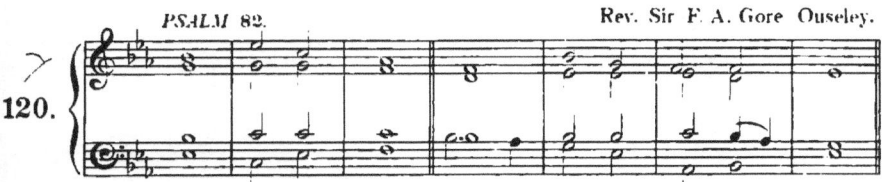

120. PSALM 82.   Rev. Sir F. A. Gore Ouseley.

121. PSALM 83.   George Cooper.

122. PSALM 84.   Dr. Stainer.

123. PSALM 85.   D. Purcell.

SEVENTEENTH DAY.

MORNING PRAYER.

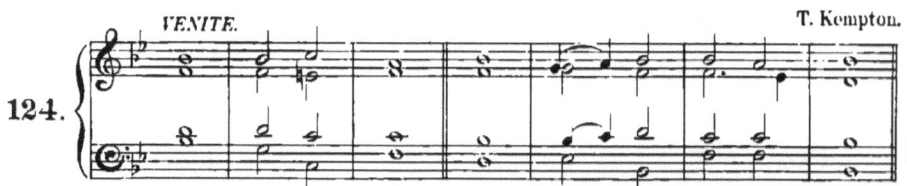

124. VENITE. T. Kempton.

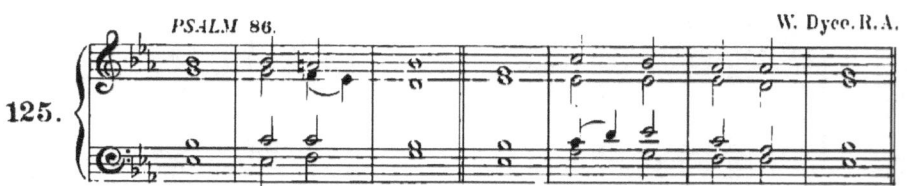

125. PSALM 86. W. Dyce, R.A.

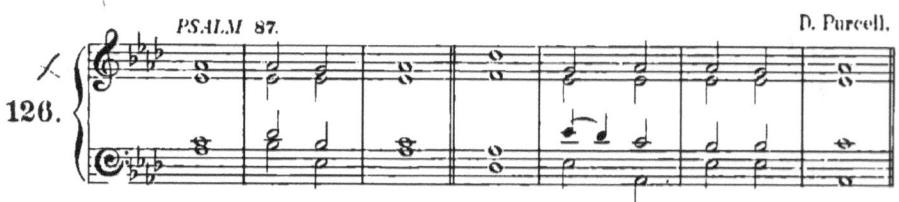

126. PSALM 87. D. Purcell.

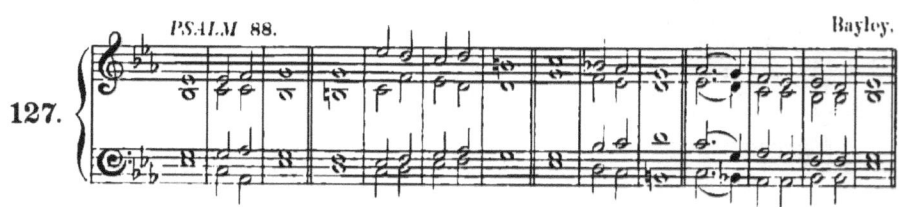

127. PSALM 88. Bayley.

SEVENTEENTH DAY.

EVENING PRAYER.

128. PSALM 59 v. 1 to 36.   J. Turle.

129. Verses 37 to 50.   Adapted from Henry Purcell by J. Turle.

Gloria to Nº 128.

EIGHTEENTH DAY.

MORNING PRAYER.

130.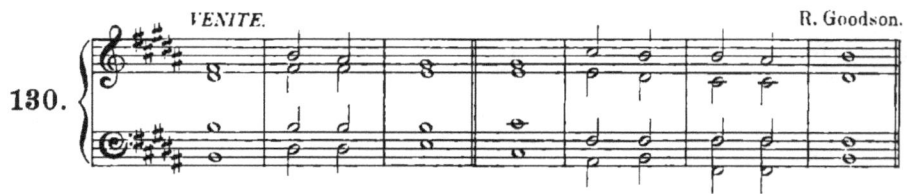

131.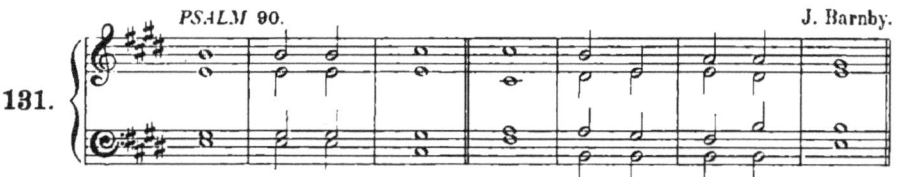

132.

133.

134.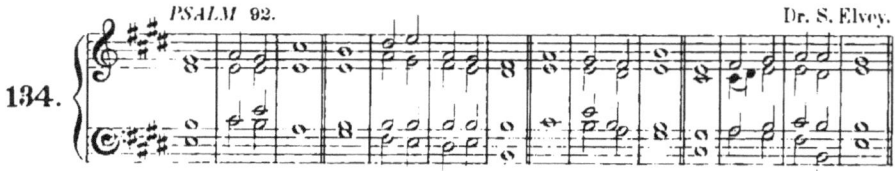

EIGHTEENTH DAY.

EVENING PRAYER.

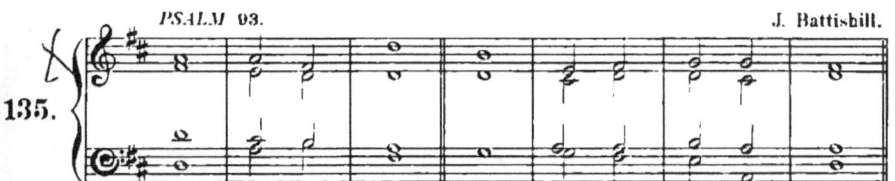

135. PSALM 93. — J. Battishill.

136. PSALM 94 v. 1 to 21. — Dr. W. Croft.

137. Verses 22 to end. — J. Battishill.

NINETEENTH DAY.

MORNING PRAYER.

138. PSALM 95. Tallis.

139. PSALM 96. G. Woodward.

140. PSALM 97. Dr. E. F. Rimbault.

NINETEENTH DAY.

EVENING PRAYER.

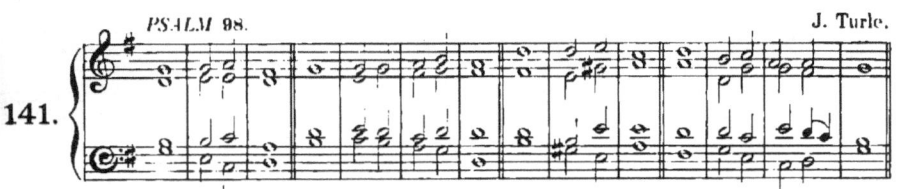

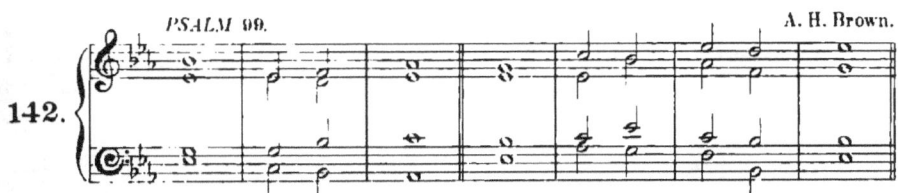

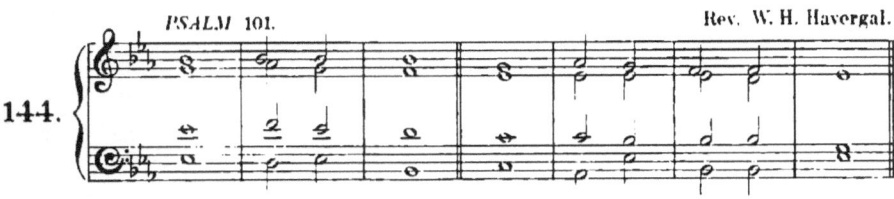

TWENTIETH DAY.

MORNING PRAYER.

145. *VENITE.* — Tallis.

146. PSALM 102 v. 1 to 11. — J. T. Cooper.

147. Verses 12 to 22. — Sir John Goss.

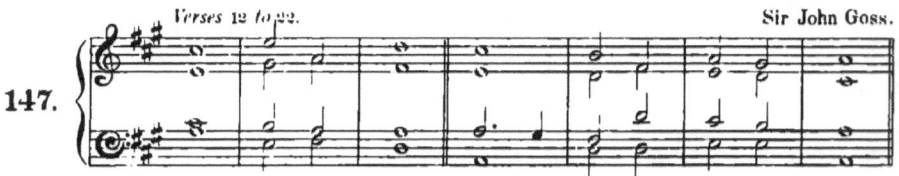

148. Verses 23 to end. — Prof. G. A. Macfarren.

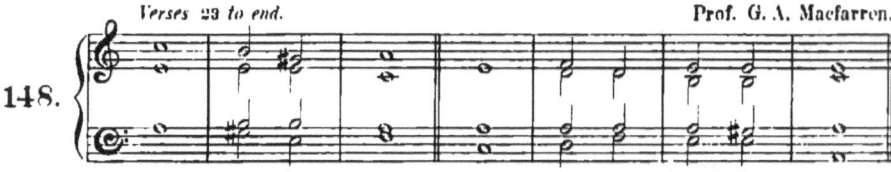

149. PSALM 103. — Sir John Goss.

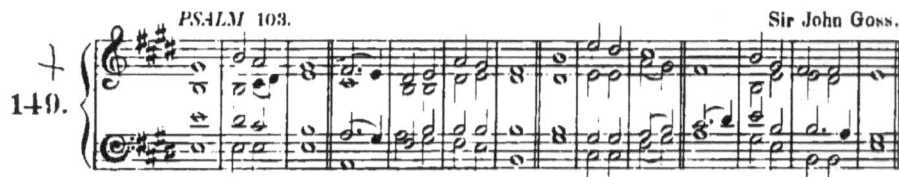

TWENTIETH DAY.

EVENING PRAYER.

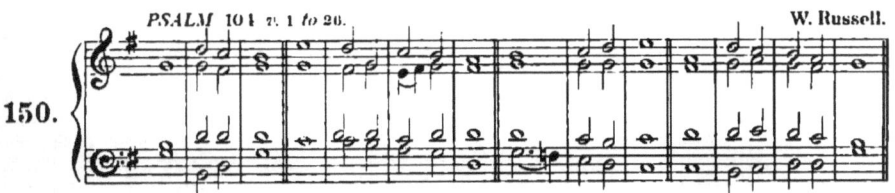

150. PSALM 104 v. 1 to 26. — W. Russell.

151. Verses 27 to 30. — Sir H. S. Oakley.

152. Verses 31 to end. — P. Fussell.

TWENTY-FIRST DAY.

MORNING PRAYER.

153.

154.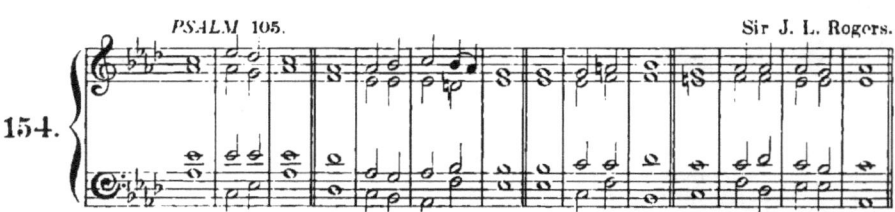

TWENTY-FIRST DAY.

EVENING PRAYER.

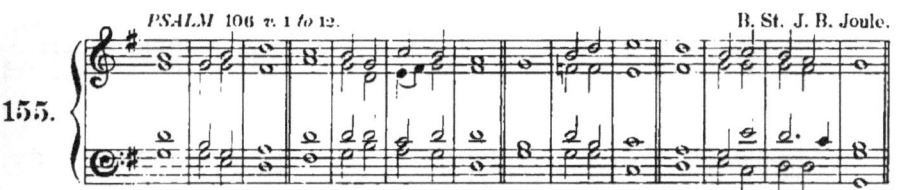

155. PSALM 106 v. 1 to 12.   B. St. J. B. Joule.

156. Verses 13 to 42.   Sir J. L. Rogers.

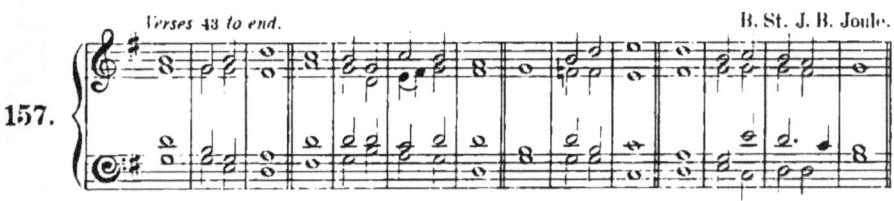

157. Verses 43 to end.   B. St. J. B. Joule.

TWENTY-SECOND DAY.

MORNING PRAYER.

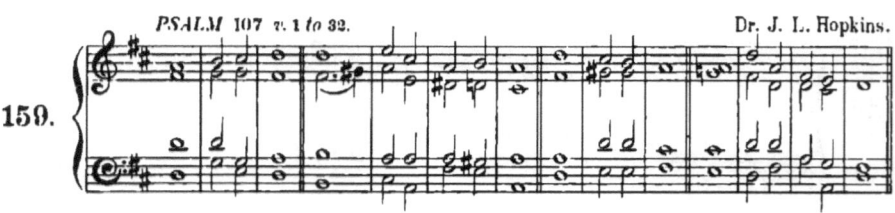

Gloria to Nº 159.

TWENTY-SECOND DAY.

EVENING PRAYER.

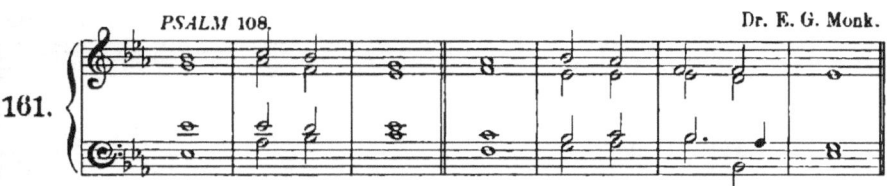
161. PSALM 108. Dr. E. G. Monk.

162. PSALM 109 v. 1 to 19. Weldon.

163. Verses 20 to 28. A. H. Brown.

164. Verses 29 to end. F. Kinkee.

TWENTY-THIRD DAY.

MORNING PRAYER.

165. VENITE. W. Savage.

166. PSALM 110. W. Dyce, R. A.

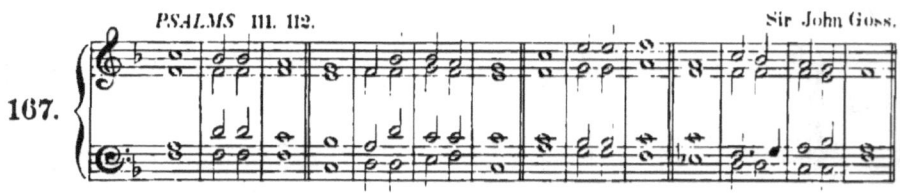

167. PSALMS 111. 112. Sir John Goss.

168. PSALM 113. H. Lawes.

TWENTY-THIRD DAY.

EVENING PRAYER.

PSALMS 114. 115.   Rev. W. Jacobs.

169.

TWENTY-FOURTH DAY.

MORNING PRAYER.

TWENTY-FOURTH DAY.

EVENING PRAYER.

175. PSALM 119 v. 1 to 24.   B. St. J. B. Joule.

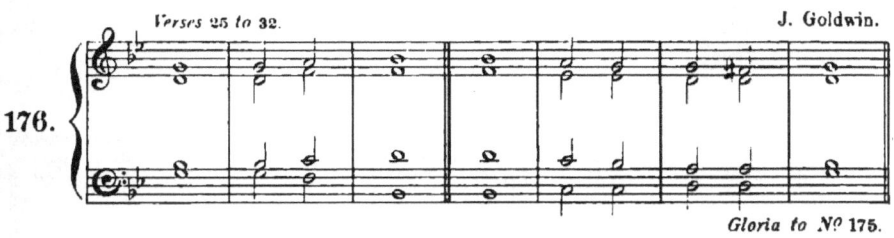

176. Verses 25 to 32.   J. Goldwin.

Gloria to N.º 175.

TWENTY-FIFTH DAY.

MORNING PRAYER.

177. VENITE. S. Webbe.

178. PSALM 119 v. 33 to 56. Sir John Goss.

179. Verses 57 to end. Henry Smart.

TWENTY-FIFTH DAY.

EVENING PRAYER.

180.
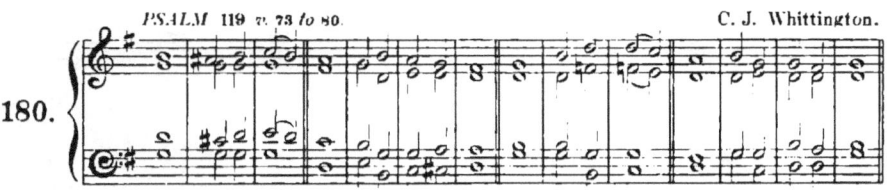

181.

182.
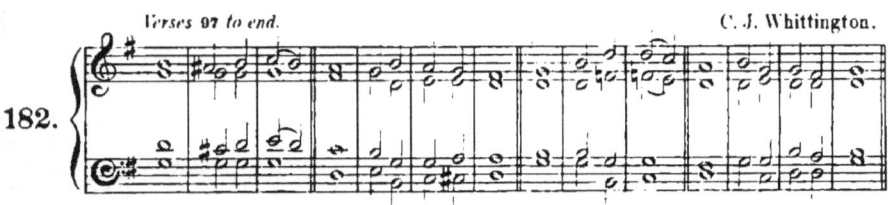

TWENTY-SIXTH DAY.

MORNING PRAYER.

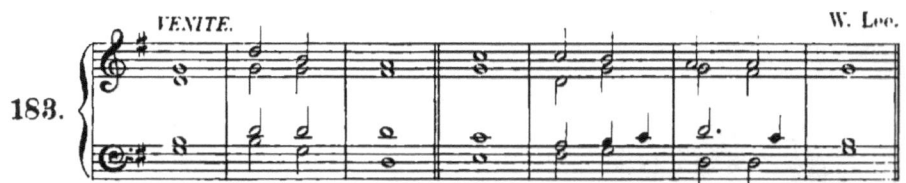

183. VENITE. W. Lee.

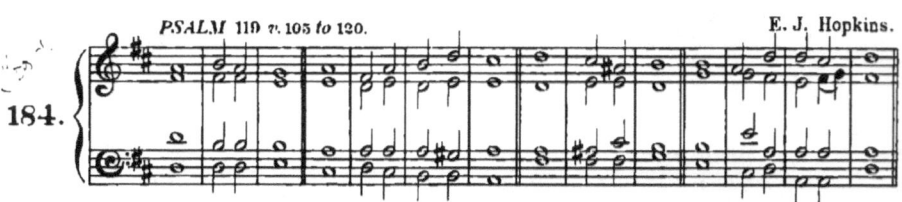

184. PSALM 119 v. 105 to 120. E. J. Hopkins.

185. Verses 121 to 128. Medley.

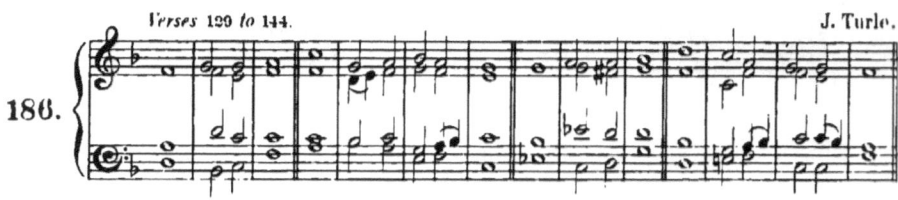

186. Verses 129 to 144. J. Turle.

TWENTY-SIXTH DAY.

EVENING PRAYER.

187. PSALM 119. v. 145 to 160. — M. Camidge.

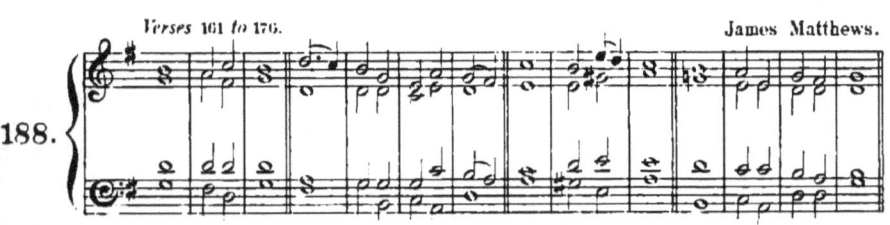

188. Verses 161 to 176. — James Matthews.

TWENTY-SEVENTH DAY.

MORNING PRAYER.

189.

190.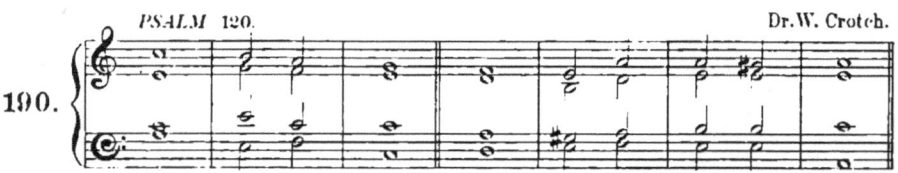

191.

192.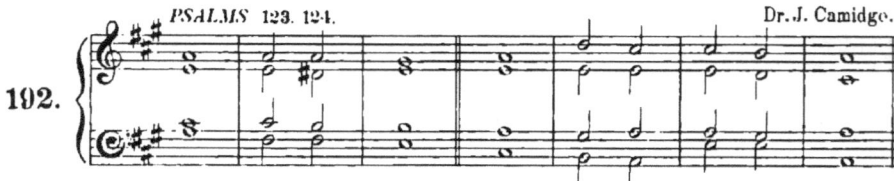

193.

TWENTY-SEVENTH DAY.

EVENING PRAYER.

194. PSALMS 126. 127.   W. Dyce. R. A.

195. PSALMS 128. 129.   T. Purcell.

196. PSALMS 130. 131.   T. Purcell.

Final Gloria to No 195.

TWENTY-EIGHTH DAY.

MORNING PRAYER.

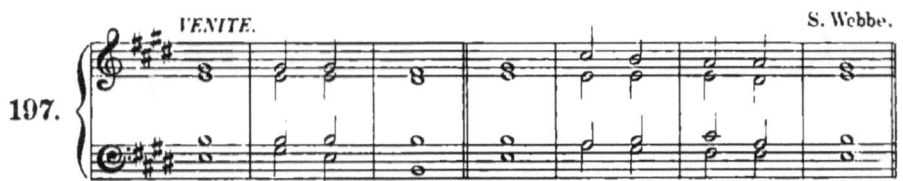

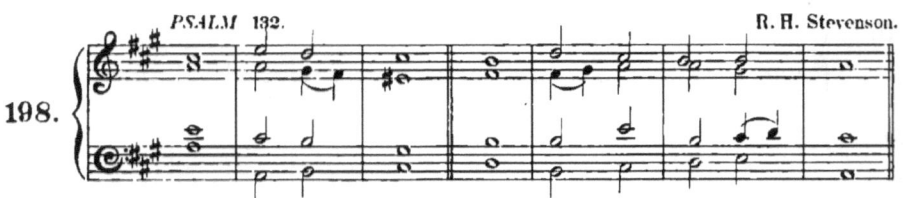

TWENTY-EIGHTH DAY.

EVENING PRAYER.

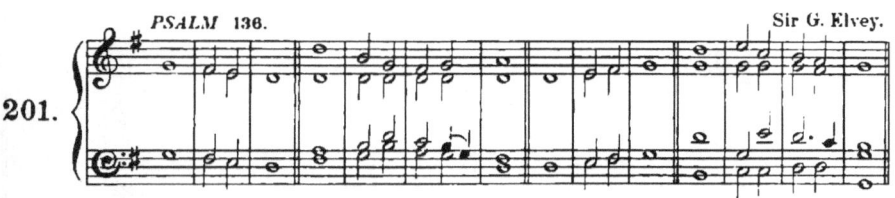

201. PSALM 136. Sir G. Elvey.

202. PSALM 137. T. Purcell.

203. PSALM 138. T. Purcell.

H

TWENTY-NINTH DAY.

MORNING PRAYER.

TWENTY-NINTH DAY.

EVENING PRAYER.

THIRTIETH DAY.

MORNING PRAYER.

210.

211.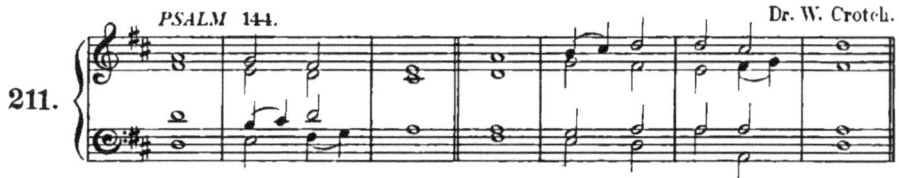

212.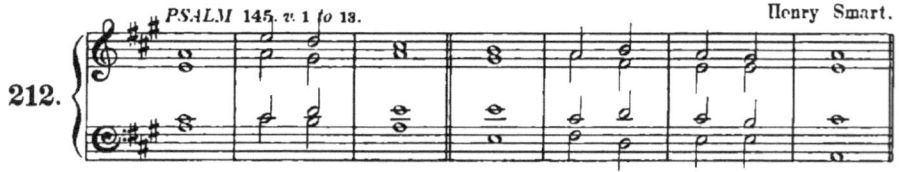

213.

214.

THIRTIETH DAY.

EVENING PRAYER.

CHRISTMAS DAY.

MORNING PRAYER.

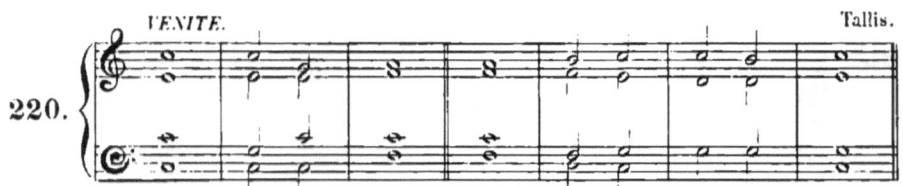

220. VENITE. Tallis.

221. PSALM 19. Isaac Barrow.

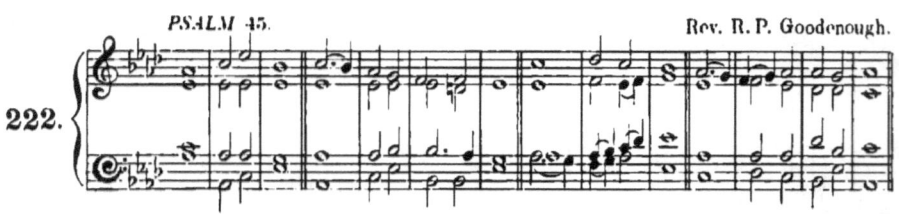

222. PSALM 45. Rev. R. P. Goodenough.

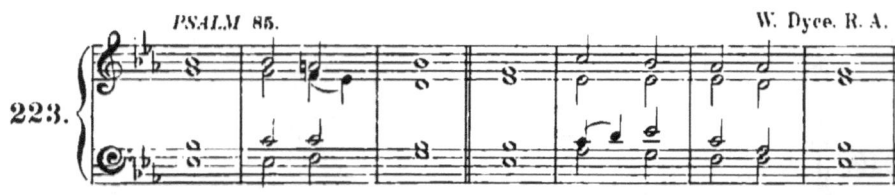

223. PSALM 85. W. Dyce. R. A.

CHRISTMAS DAY.

EVENING PRAYER.

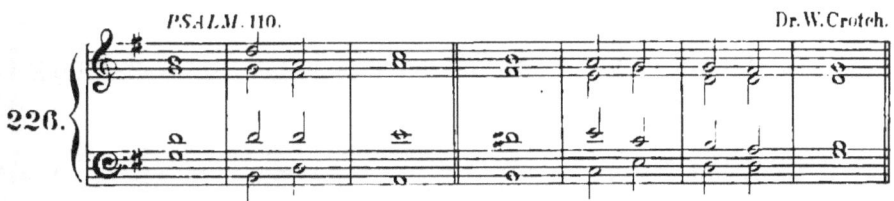

ASH-WEDNESDAY.

MORNING PRAYER.

228. VENITE. — C. E. Stephens.

229. PSALM 6. — J. Battishill.

230. PSALM 32. — Longdon.

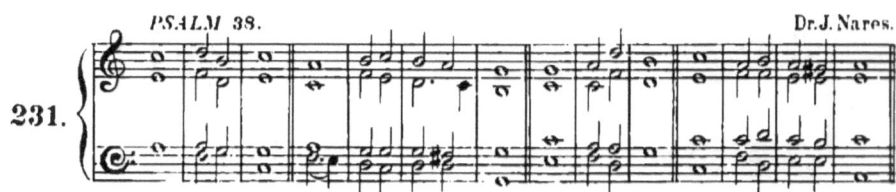

231. PSALM 38. — Dr. J. Nares.

ASH WEDNESDAY.

EVENING PRAYER.

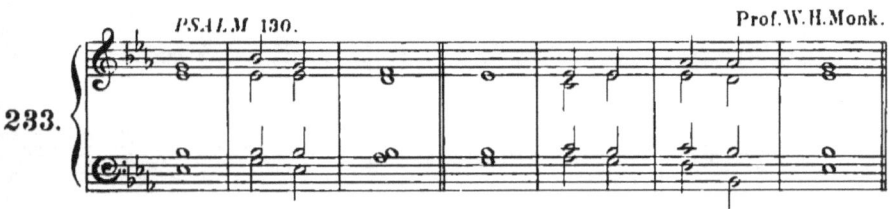

GOOD FRIDAY.

MORNING PRAYER.

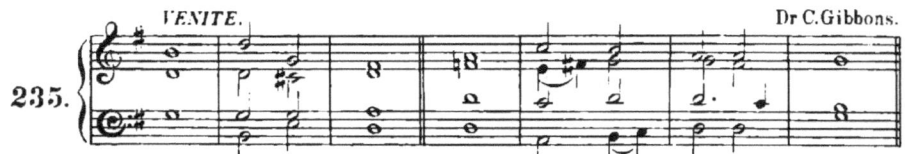

235. VENITE. — Dr C. Gibbons.

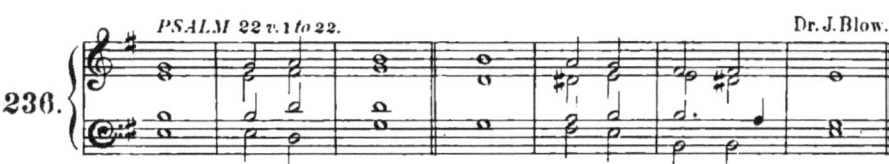

236. PSALM 22 v. 1 to 22. — Dr. J. Blow.

237. Verses 23 to end. — Dr. J. Blow.

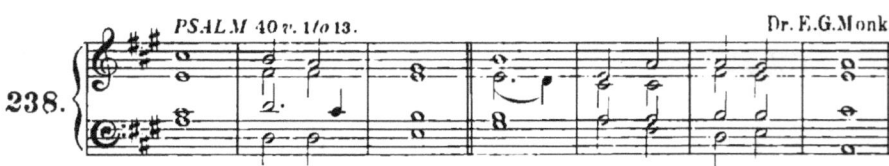

238. PSALM 40 v. 1 to 13. — Dr. E. G. Monk.

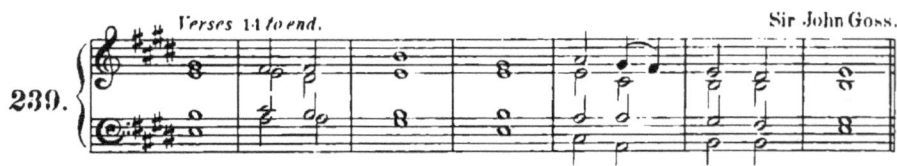

239. Verses 14 to end. — Sir John Goss.

240. PSALM 54. — A. H. Brown.

GOOD FRIDAY.

EVENING PRAYER.

EASTER DAY.

MORNING PRAYER.

EASTER DAY.

EVENING PRAYER.

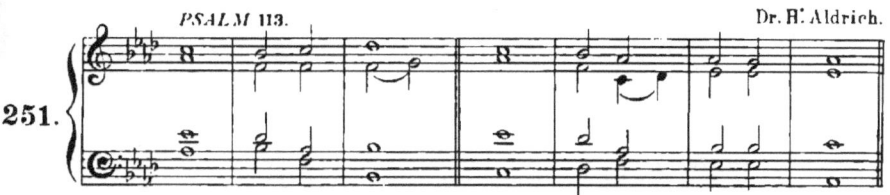

251. PSALM 113. — Dr. H. Aldrich.

252. PSALM 114. — J. Turle.

253. PSALM 118. — A. H. Brown.

ASCENSION DAY.

MORNING PRAYER.

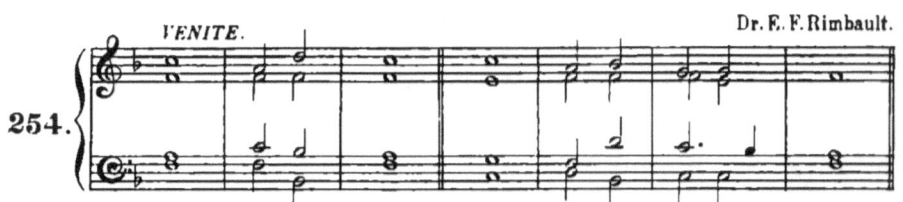

254. VENITE. Dr. E. F. Rimbault.

255. PSALM 8. Dr. E. G. Monk.

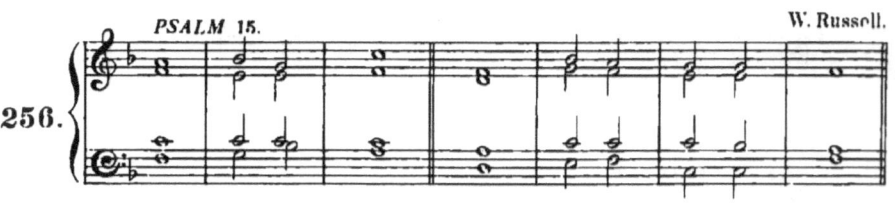

256. PSALM 15. W. Russell.

257. PSALM 21. Sir G. Elvey.

ASCENSION DAY.

EVENING PRAYER.

258. PSALM 24.   Sir G. Elvey.

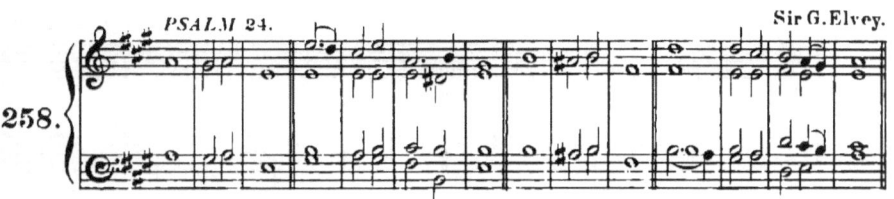

259. PSALM 47.   Dr. W. Crotch.

260. PSALM 108.   D. Purcell.

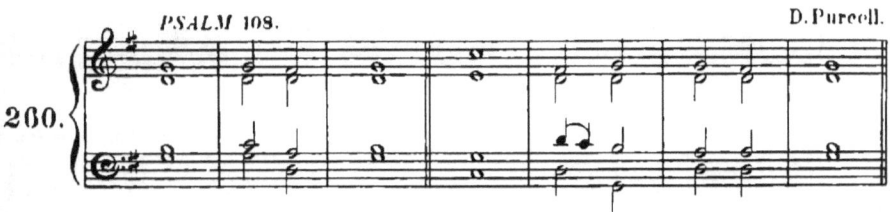

WHIT SUNDAY.

MORNING PRAYER.

261. VENITE. — Sir G. Elvey.

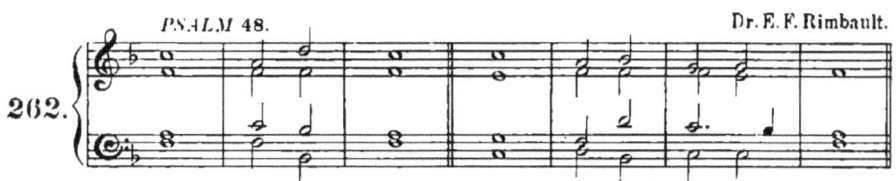

262. PSALM 48. — Dr. E. F. Rimbault.

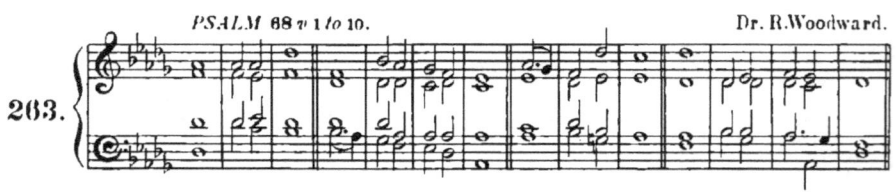

263. PSALM 68 v 1 to 10. — Dr. R. Woodward.

264. Verses 11 to 20. — Rev. J. Troutbeck.

265. Verses 21 to end. — Earl of Mornington.

WHIT SUNDAY.

EVENING PRAYER.

266. PSALM 104 v. 1 to 26. — J. Turle.

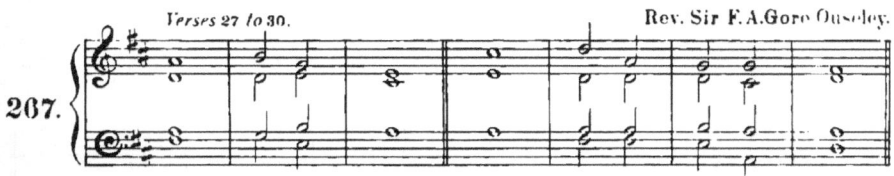

267. Verses 27 to 30. — Rev. Sir F. A. Gore Ouseley.

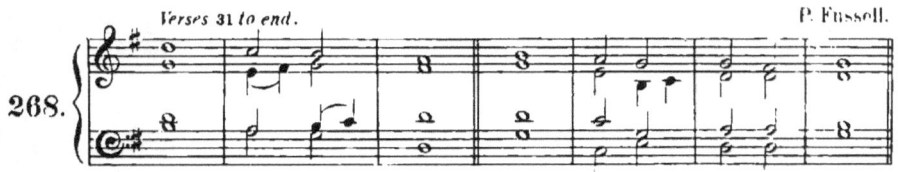

268. Verses 31 to end. — P. Fussell.

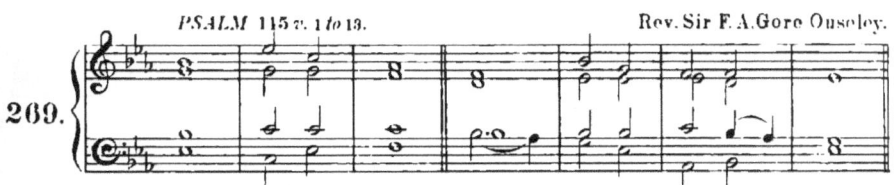

269. PSALM 115 v. 1 to 13. — Rev. Sir F. A. Gore Ouseley.

270. Verses 14 to 21. — Dr. J. Camidge.

HARVEST FESTIVAL.

Psalms 65. 67. 150.

271. PSALM 65. — Dr. J. L. Hopkins.

272. PSALM 67. — Sir J. L. Rogers.

273. PSALM 150. Verses 1 and 2. — P. Humphreys.

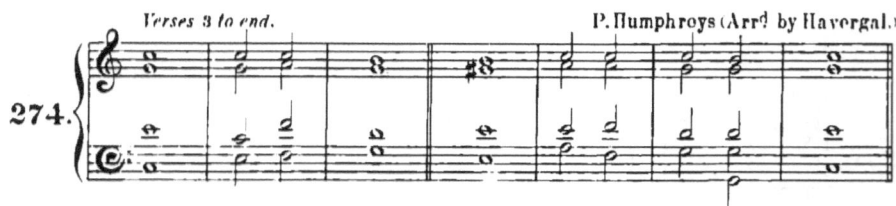

274. Verses 3 to end. — P. Humphreys (Arr? by Havergal.)

NEW YEAR'S EVE.

Psalms 39.90.

275.

276.

277.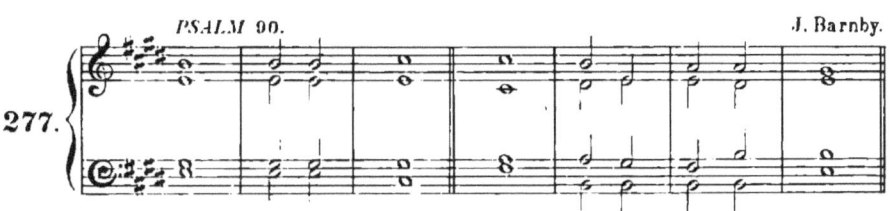

SOLEMNIZATION OF MATRIMONY.

BURIAL OF THE DEAD.

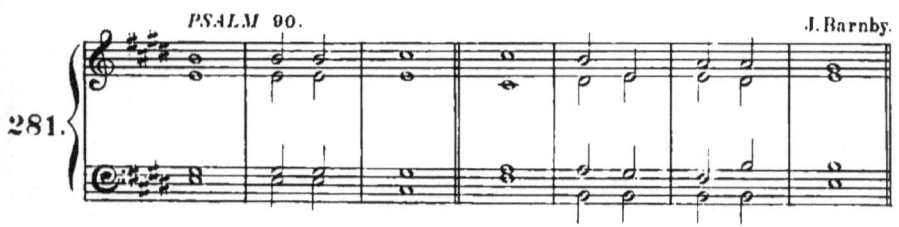

BENEDICTUS.

Rev. W. H. Havergal.

282.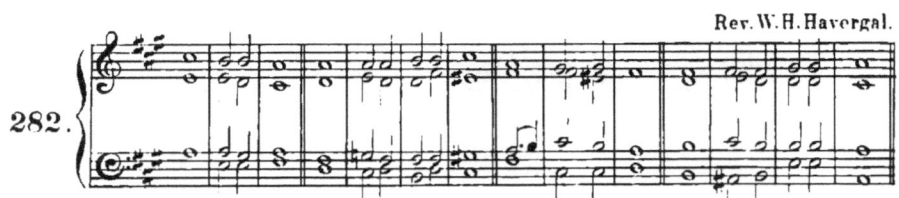

Fountain Meen.

283.

Adapted from Spohr
by J. Turle.

284.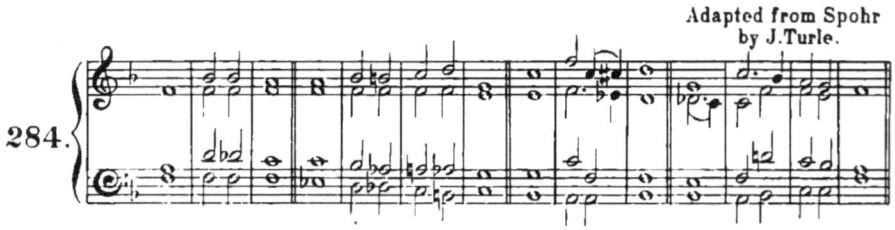

J. Matthews.

285.

JUBILATE.

JUBILATE.

MAGNIFICAT.

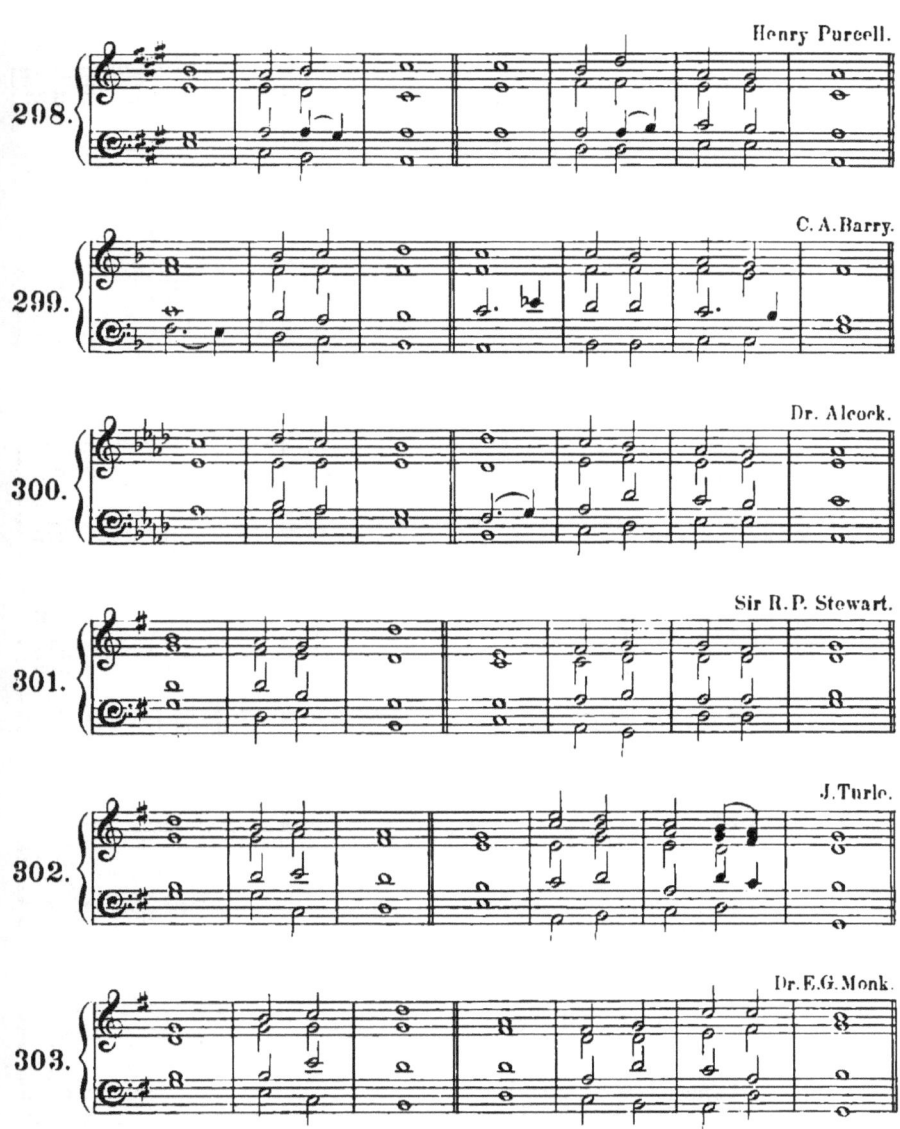

MAGNIFICAT.

MAGNIFICAT.

CANTATE DOMINO.

CANTATE DOMINO.

NUNC DIMITTIS.

NUNC DIMITTIS.

NUNC DIMITTIS.

QUICUNQUE VULT.
(Tallis.)
Arranged by Arthur Henry Brown.

344.

www.ingramcontent.com/pod-product-compliance
Lightning Source LLC
Chambersburg PA
CBHW020151170426
43199CB00010B/988